ALONG *the* RIVER III
DARK VOICES FROM THE RIO GRANDE

edited by
DAVID BOWLES

VAO Publishing
A division of *Valley Artistic Outreach*
4717 N FM 493
Donna, TX 78537
www.vaopublishing.com

ISBN: 978-0615956183

First printed edition: January 2014

TABLE *of* CONTENTS

FOREWARD
PROSE SELECTIONS

1   Niño—Álvaro Rodríguez
3   The Hostel/La hostería—Alejandro Cabada Fernández
10 La Bruja del Rancho—Brianda Salinas
13 La Casa de Muchos Ojos—Mario E. Martínez
18 Lucky Family of the Decade/Orphic Easter Egg—
    Angelo Bowles
29 Las Voces del Llano—Evangelina Ayon
31 Sunsets/The Little Girl—Tiffany Cano
37 Nobody Remembers Dying/Lady Lechuza—Alyssa Aide Vela
45 Las Lechuzas de Falfurrias/What I Know of Mariposas—
    Priscilla Celina Suárez
50 Missed Connection—Anna Solís
51 Little Tickle—Magaly García
54 J.J. and the Cucuy/Huevos a la Ranchera—Nina Medrano
60 Todo Está Bien—Marianita Escamilla
64 The Lightning Storm—William Mainous II
68 Driving through Spotlights/Before I Paint—Diana Elizondo
71 An Angeleno's Assimilation into Harlingen—
    Susanna Groves
75 Important Chickens (and a Bird) from My Life/Striding the
    Border/Vestige to Visage—Juventino Manzano
97 Bringing down the Witch—David Bowles

DRAMA SELECTION

109 Night by the River—Michael Verderber

POETRY SELECTIONS

127 That Night—Amy Cummins
128 Lynx in October/In the Bedroom/Melancholia/Existential Thanatos—Alejandro Cabada Fernández
144 The Inbetween/What Goes Bump in the Night/Carrion Flower/My Tenants—Alexandra Sepúlveda
149 A River's Tale—Johanna Ríos
151 Surprises from the Grave/Pepe Who Didn't Know—Priscilla Celina Suárez
156 Echoplex/Keeper of Flies/The Dorian Gray of Her Time—Anna L. Solís
159 The Resurrection/Demons—William Mainous II
161 Violent Specter/Vampire Kingdom/Jack O'Lanterns/To Poe—Diana Elizondo
165 The Gods Are Funny That Way #6—Chuck Taylor
166 blue 'n' brown is brown/At the Park—Juventino Manzano
168 Why I'm Becoming Catholic—Nina Medrano
170 Crow, Buzzard, Hummingbirds—David Bowles

CONTRIBUTOR BIOGRAPHIES

FOREWORD

VAO Publishing believes that people in our community need venues for their artistic expression. It is essential that human beings have a creative outlet for their dreams, emotions, ideas. A life without art is somehow poorer, so the small regional press works to provide opportunities for self-expression.

The present volume is the third in VAO Publishing's *Along the River* anthology series, a project that showcases the diverse writing talent of south Texas, sampling the language and literature of this region, its peculiar rhythms and accents, the rich culture that it so eloquently encodes. For the first time we have asked writers to submit work that fits the theme *dark voices*, as we wish to celebrate the region's long-standing tradition of frightening folktales and urban legends.

The contributors to *Along the River III* range from established authors to emerging talents, from professors to students, from computer technicians to retirees and everything in between. Just as varied as the authors are the pieces themselves, a comingling of prose, poetry and drama that seeks to shine light on the gloom-laden secret places of our culture and our hearts. For when the sun sets on the Río Grande Valley, all manner of dark voices begin to croak, snarl and wail. Led by the voices of *abuelitos y tías*, the writers in this volume want to take you by the hand and explore the black shadows amidst the mesquite and palm trees down at the water's edge...but be careful not to fall—or be pulled—into the current!

In addition to its importance for the burgeoning literary scene in the Río Grande Valley and its environs, this anthology is also an important tool in the promotion of the arts throughout our region. VAO Publishing's parent organization, Valley Artistic Outreach, was founded in 2010, by a group of artists driven by a shared vision: go into communities throughout the Río Grande Valley and provide art workshops to kids who—because of their socio-economic status or because their schools had abandoned the arts to focus on state testing—had no access to the sorts of horizon-expanding activities that tend to put more affluent students at a distinct advantage.

This mission has resulted in our collaboration with partners throughout the RGV to carry out arts workshops (and to host multiple art exhibits and performances, providing venues for the artistic expression of adults as well). In a time in which federal and state funding for the arts is at a historic low, this anthology series can be a boon to artists and children. With the proceeds from the sale of *Along the River III*, VAO will continue its dual mission, helping to nourish the seed that the arts can plant in the heart of every member of our community.

By purchasing the book you hold in your hands, you have become a partner in that very worthy endeavor. Thanks!

DAVID BOWLES
JANUARY 1, 2014

PROSE

SELECTIONS

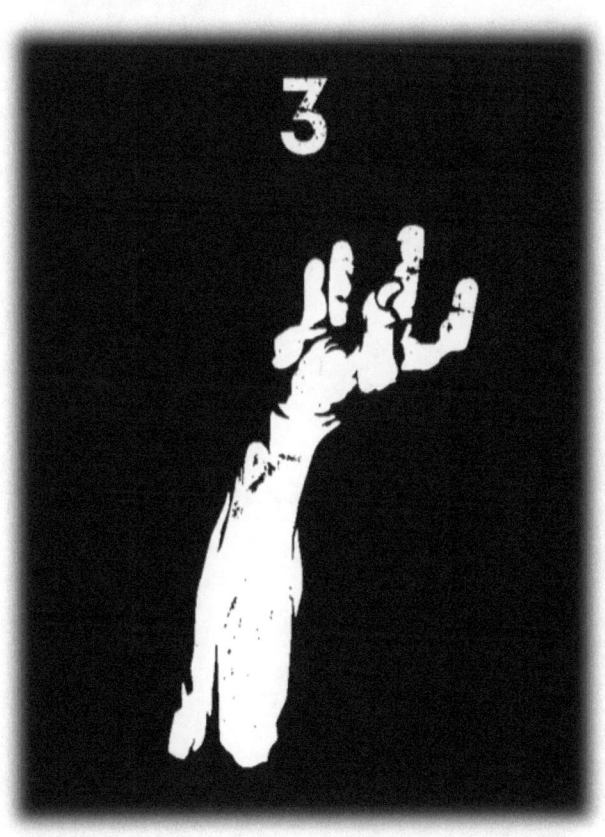

NIÑO

It was her first baby and they named him Aurelio, after his father and his grandfather.

It was born in the backseat of the Oldsmobile because they couldn't get to the hospital in time and Aurelio delivered his son himself.

He was a beautiful boy, about seven pounds if they had to guess but no one could be sure, from the top of the head to the shoulders, elbows and arms. But the baby's trunk devolved into a spray of tentacles like a squid's, oozy and coiling and uncoiling. Aurelio wrapped the boy in a beach towel, tight, so he couldn't squirm so much.

Then they drove home and walked inside and shut the door behind them, locking it.

Two weeks later, they took it to the little church to be baptized. It was just a squat baptismal font made out of wood and copper sheeting, with a basin to dip a bowl in sprinkle God's rain on the baby's pate. Aurelio agreed to do this because of the manner of baptism. He would not have allowed the baby to be dunked in the water for fear it would break loose and swim away like a fugitive from an aquarium.

Maritza, the boy's mother at eighteen, cried bitterly each time she put her tit to the baby's mouth and he refused it with salty tears. Finally, Aurelio went to the dollar store and found some fish paste that could be watered down and the child sucked it down rabidly.

Aurelio knew it had been blessed and would go to heaven and with Maritza's consent, he wrapped the baby in its beach towel and drove out away from the house down a dirt road under the moonlight.

He set to digging a small pit under a mesquite tree, then crisscrossed branches and dried twigs into a crib, got the charcoal starter from the trunk and doused the nest and laid the bundle on top, squirting out the last of it. He was suddenly seized by an idea and rewrapped the child in aluminum foil.

He lit a match and threw it in.

It burned for the better part of an hour, and smelled good and bad at the same time.

When the embers had died down to ashes, he took a fork and began to pry the thing out of the hole. He set it on the ground in front of the Olds' headlights and peeled away the foil.

The rainbow was reflected in his face. The bones had turned to jewels: rubies, emeralds, sapphires; and gold and pearls. It was like a safety deposit box had been opened in the desert. And there were stacks of money underneath, wrapped in bundles of fifties, hundreds. And at the very bottom, an XBOX 360, without the box.

ÁLVARO RODRÍGUEZ

THE HOSTEL

The drops of water splattered violently, as if the skies were spitting hammers against the hood of my car. I'd been driving for hours, and the night seemed to grow darker and darker. My head squirmed with memories. I'd always been faithful to my ideals, to my family, to my wife...Why would she do this to me? The simple act of recalling her face took me back to the moment when I found her with another man. The bitch. I'd decided to get lost deep in the heart of Europe just to get away from her. I needed to escape my tormented past and get my head straight. Maybe try to remake my life. The bitch.

In the distance I made out a neon sign that read *Herberge-Hostel*. Since it was madness to keep driving into the jaws of this storm, I decided to stop at the inn.

My German wasn't great, but I could make myself understood. Without much difficulty, I rented a room and went to get some rest. As I walked down the long hall that led to the room, I noticed that in the middle of the foyer a beautiful woman was relaxing on a black velvet chaise longue. Her pale skin was a flawless landscape surely crafted by the Teutonic gods themselves, her hair a stampede of black coursers that slipped down neck and shoulders until they covered her docile breast.

I had glanced at her discretely, taking care not to leer, but I did greet her with cordial eyes, and she nodded with a smile. I quickened my stride, ducking into my room to freshen up before immediately returning to the foyer to meet the lovely woman.

Our evening was a welcome surprise. Not only was she beautiful; she was also sophisticated and quite intelligent. Our conversation touched on many subjects, like the evolution of Mexican cinema and German expressionism in films like *The Cabinet of Doctor Caligari*. We agreed on everything! She was the perfect woman, and she was all mine.

There we were, all alone well after 2 am. We'd shared several bottles of wine, and the alcohol had set our blood aflame. Her long fingers caressed my face and lost themselves in my hair. I stared at her with the eyes of a hungry predator just before it rips into its prey, and she, ecstatic, extended an invitation. The inevitable attack was set into motion: I pounced on her lips to consume that immoral mouth. But despite her dazzling beauty, her lips were like sandpaper, and her long, sticky tongue swirled strangely in my mouth.

Suddenly, I felt a pricking sensation on my palate, and my saliva glands kicked in as I tasted bitter blood flooding my mouth. Startled, I pushed the woman away and stood, staring at her in consternation. Her lips were smeared with my blood.

My pulse quickened. I didn't really understand what was going on. I was frightened, but what made my skin crawl was watching her flick out a bifurcated tongue and lick with two rapid movements the scarlet liquid that covered her mouth. I bolted for my room and locked myself in. Overcome, I dropped to my knees on the carpet, trying to understand what had just happened.

"It must be the alcohol," I told myself aloud, and then, without realizing, I fell asleep.

I DON' T KNOW how much time went by, but when I opened my eyes I felt paralyzed, naked and defenseless, suffused with a feeling of horror. Hundreds of serpents slithered all about me and under my back. The darkness devoured the walls of the room, and the only sound was this hissing of the deadly reptiles. I felt weak, confused, drugged—I couldn't coordinate my movements and my pores were flooded by sweat. Suddenly I saw an enormous silhouette that climbed with great caution atop my body. I could feel black tresses upon my face, and I understood that it was the woman from the foyer. But she was no longer a seductress. What squatted on me felt like a heavy, scaly blob that rubbed itself strangely against my chest. I struggled to move, to get away from the thing, that being that held me down, but my strength had ebbed away completely.

The ambient temperature changed. It became a humid heat that smothered me, thrusting me deeper into delirium. The thing atop me panted uncontrollably, its breathing hoarse like the grunts of beasts rutting at dawn. I found myself petrified, consumed by fear at the uncertainty of my survival. It was in that instant that some sort of stinger stabbed like a bayonet into my genitals. The pain was sharp, wrenching a screech of pain from me as a veritable red sea spilled itself out between my legs. I felt my death approach as I realized my flesh was being spitted like a martyr run through by a lance.

THE NEXT MORNING I heard police sirens just outside the hostel. I got out of bed, completely intact, as if nothing had happened. Rushing outside, I saw a car, identical to mine, smashed to bits and partially embedded in a huge true. Panic once again surged within as I saw that the driver was lying dead, head smashed, covered in blood...impaled cruelly upon a gigantic tree limb.

In the trunk, the police discovered the mutilated body of a black-haired woman, covered in hundreds of writhing serpents. No one seemed to see me. I walked away in search of new shelter.

ALEJANDRO CABADA FERNÁNDEZ

[TRANSLATED BY DAVID BOWLES]

LA HOSTERÍA

L as gotas de agua caían con violencia como si el cielo escupiera martillos sobre el capacete de mi auto. Llevaba horas manejando y la noche parecía hacerse cada vez más negra. Mi cabeza era un hormiguero de recuerdos. Siempre fui fiel a mis ideales, a mi familia, a mi mujer, ¿por qué me pagaba de esa manera? El simple hecho de recordar su mirada me transportaba al instante mismo en que la encontré con otro hombre. Maldita. Alejarme de ella, era el motivo por el que había decidido internarme en el centro de Europa. Tenía que huir de mi pasado tormentoso y poner mis pensamientos en orden. Quizá intentar rehacer mi vida. Maldita. A lo lejos vi un letrero iluminado que decía *Herberge-Hostel* y viendo que era imposible manejar contra las fauces de la tormenta, decidí detenerme en ese hostal.

Mi alemán no era muy bueno, pero podía darme a entender. Sin batallar mucho alquilé un cuarto y me dirigí a descansar. Al caminar por el largo pasillo que conducía a las habitaciones, me percaté que en medio del vestíbulo había una mujer muy hermosa sentada en un gran sillón de terciopelo negro. Su piel pálida era un paisaje molecular que los mismos dioses teutones debieron haber diseñado y una estampida de corceles negros deslizaba por su larga cabellera hasta cubrir sus dóciles pechos. La vi con discreción sin insinuarme de forma ordinaria, pero sí la saludé con una mirada cordial y ella asintió con una sonrisa. De prisa entré en mi habitación para asearme un poco y de inmediato regresé al vestíbulo para conocer a la bella mujer.

La velada resultó una grata sorpresa. La mujer no sólo era hermosa, sino que era también sofisticada y muy inteligente. Tocamos diversos temas, como la evolución del cine en México y el expresionismo del cine alemán en *El gabinete del doctor Caligari* ¡Coincidíamos en todo! Era la mujer perfecta y era toda para mí. Estábamos solos, ya eran más de las dos de la madrugada y después de varias botellas de vino, el alcohol había empezado a enardecer la sangre. Sus largas manos acariciaban mi rostro y se perdían entre mi cabello. Yo la veía con ojos de depredador hambriento justo antes de despedazar a su presa y ella, estática, me extendía la invitación. Sucedió lo inevitable y me lancé vorazmente sobre sus labios para consumir su boca inmoral. A pesar de ser una mujer de belleza deslumbrante, sus labios eran como lijas y su lengua era larga, pegajosa y daba giros muy peculiares dentro de mi boca. De pronto, sentí un piquete en el paladar y mis glándulas salivales se alteraron al probar la sangre amarga que invadía mi boca. Sobresaltado, empujé a la mujer y me levanté del sillón. La observé desconcertado. Vi su boca cubierta de mi sangre. Mi pulso se aceleró, no entendía bien lo que estaba pasando. Estaba aterrado, pero lo que me erizó la piel fue al ver cómo sacó su lengua bífida y en dos movimientos lamió el líquido escarlata que cubría sus labios. Salí disparado rumbo a mi habitación y me encerré. Agitado, caí de rodillas sobre la alfombra tratando de entender qué era lo que había sucedido. Tiene que ser el alcohol, me dije en voz alta y, sin darme cuenta, me quedé dormido.

No sé cuánto tiempo pasó, pero al abrir los ojos me sentí paralizado, desnudo e indefenso, invadido por una sensación espeluznante. Cientos de serpientes se arrastraban a mi alrededor y por debajo de mi espalda. La oscuridad devoraba las paredes de la habitación y sólo podía escuchar el sisear de los reptiles mortíferos. Me sentía débil, confundido, drogado, no podía coordinar mis movimientos y el sudor ahogaba mis poros. De pronto, vi una silueta enorme que, con sutileza, se echó encima de mi cuerpo. Pude sentir sus mechones negros sobre mi rostro y comprendí que era la mujer del vestíbulo. Pero ya no era la mujer seductora. Lo que estaba encima de mí se sentía como un pesado bulto escamoso que se frotaba de forma extraña sobre mi pecho. Luchaba por moverme, por escapar de ese bulto, ese ser que me oprimía, pero mi fuerza me había abandonado. La temperatura en mi entorno cambió. Era un calor húmedo que me asfixiaba y me adentraba más en mi delirio. El ser jadeaba desenfrenado, su respiración era ronca como la voz de las bestias apareándose al amanecer. Me vi petrificado, consumido por el miedo ante la incertidumbre de mi vida. Fue en ese instante que sentí un aguijón que se clavaba como una bayoneta sobre mis genitales. El dolor era agudo y dejé escapar un grito de terror al momento que el mar rojo del *Éxodo* se desbordaba entre mis piernas. Me sentí morir al entender que mi carne estaba siendo perforada igual que la de un mártir al ser atravesado por una lanza.

A la mañana siguiente escuché sirenas de patrullas justo a las afueras del hostal. Me levanté intacto, como si nada hubiera pasado. Salí corriendo al ver un auto idéntico al mío hecho pedazos incrustado contra un árbol enorme. Una vez más el pánico invadió mi cuerpo al ver que el conductor del auto yacía muerto, su cráneo fracturado, bañado en sangre... inmolado cruelmente por una rama gigantesca. En la cajuela, los oficiales de la policía encontraron el cuerpo mutilado de una mujer de cabellos negros cubierta por un centenar de serpientes. Nadie notó mi presencia. Me alejé caminando en busca de un nuevo albergue.

ALEJANDRO CABADA FERNÁNDEZ

LA BRUJA DEL RANCHO

Growing up on a ranch in Mexico, you hear a lot of talk about love and tragedy. Starstruck lovers and jealous rage are just a few things kids hear adults discuss. The strangest things are those unseen. For such a small area, the ranch had a lot of life with it, both living and dead. I remember walking around and knowing wherever I stood there was a story waiting to be heard. It could be something to scare the children or what you witnessed yourself. *La Bruja del Rancho* was just one of those tales that will haunt the very heart of the ranch.

She was a mystery that was left unseen. Her eyes were a temptation for the weak. Her curse was forever. No one knew exactly who she was or where she came from, but everyone knew what she did. She was a curandera, a rural healer, with a kind heart filled with love for everyone at the ranch. Using herbs and sages, she cured the poor who could not afford a doctor. They say she was beautiful, her hair dark like the night sky, each eye a different color (some even said she was actually two souls in one body), one grey like a silver wolf and the other a hue of brown. Her skin was fair and soft, which meant she never worked the labor of the ranch life. Her beauty was pure, but her name was tainted. You see, she had a reputation for sleeping around with men both married and single. People talked, but that didn't stop them from using her for their needs. She didn't care, either – until she fell in love.

He was a handsome man, muscles from labor and a smile to make anyone swoon. They fancied each other. For him it was only physical, but he didn't reveal this. Every night of passion was a step closer to her demise, but she didn't know. To her it was true love. He carelessly told her he loved her and would marry her someday. He kept her hopes high that one day she would have her happily ever after – until she saw him with another girl, Stella, at the market place.

She couldn't believe it. He was holding *her* hand, and taking *her* to the market. They were holding each other adoringly and looked happy. He was happy with *her*. La Bruja del Rancho didn't want to make a scene, so she spied on them. What was that on her left hand? *An engagement ring*! She was angry, and waited for them to depart to get a lock of Stella's hair for her own doing. La Bruja del Rancho waited until Stella was alone and her lover was out of sight. She got a lock of her hair and went about her day at the market to make her evil plans that night. She cast a spell on poor Stella, but it was not an ordinary spell; this was a pact with the devil. Our Bruja would do anything to keep her man. So she summoned the devil himself and made a pact to lose her beauty in exchange for Stella feeling the shame she made our Bruja endure.

The next morning Stella woke up to the sound of visitors in her living room. She quickly got ready and entered the room to greet them, only to feel their glares. She looked at herself in the mirror...She looked pregnant! *How can this be?* she wondered. She was a virgin and engaged to be married. She thought, *This is a dream, this is only a dream.* She could hear everyone talking about her saying things like "village whore," and "una cualquiera." She was shocked, both by her apparent pregnancy and by the very people that she called her friends calling her such things. They left but their glares remained. As soon as her visitors were gone, her belly went back to normal. This went on for a few days: only when she was around people would she appear pregnant. She stayed indoors where no one could see her. Everything was normal until her fiancé visited.

He entered the house, and on cue her stomach grew. He looked at her in disgust and said it was over. He could not marry someone who carried another man's child. She begged and pleaded that she did no such thing. But to him it was nonsense since the proof was there, and she could not disprove what was happening. He left Stella and went to the Bruja's house to seek some comfort only to be confronted by horrendous woman in her place. He left the ranch, never to be heard from again.

Stella cried herself to sleep that evening, not knowing when her day became night. In a daze she heard her stomach mocking her with a tune: "Te dejó, he left you, because you're a whore." She heard maniacal laughter coming from everywhere in that house and she could do nothing to stop the noise. *He left the whore. The whore is alone.* These words pierced her. She looked around frantically until she found a butcher knife. With no hesitation she stabbed her stomach to stop the laughter, the shame she felt, the taunting, the ache in her heart, and her life. She died alone, in that house; no one knows what happened to her body afterwards.

Rumors say someone found Stella's remains, but when they came back with help she was gone. Her fiancé had left after the embarrassment she made him go through; no one knows what happened to him. Same goes for our Bruja; no one knows what happened to her. Some say she was thrown over a cliff by the people of the ranch. Some say she died of a broken heart. If all of that is true, who was it that I saw at her house?

BRIANDA SALINAS

LA CASA DE MUCHOS OJOS

He was ready to die by fire. The storm lit up the night above Bill Black's head like a nightmare. Each bright volley bounced shadows off the clouds in horrific shapes of humanoid goats and grinning demons. His wool cap was soaked through and the muddy water he'd tramped in for miles was up to his knees, staining the hem of his coat. Booming thunder forced Bill down an aged path. For a moment, he hid under a tree and remembered once he heard that trees attracted lightning and ran off further down the overgrown lane. He planned his routes by the sporadic flashes of light and felt like he was being watched, though he knew he was the only fool running through the Texas backwoods that night.

Down a bend in the road, he fell and crawled on hands and knees away from the lightning. During the flashes, Bill spotted a ruin of a house. There was no lawn to speak of, only a boggish thicket of high grass swaying in the wind. Bill Black ran through it and fell onto his side when his slick boot hit the dry porch. He checked to see if his half-drunk bottle of tequila made the daring search for cover and laughed when he traced the edges of it in his pocket with his thick fingers.

"Ain't nothing on heaven and earth that can get the best of Bill Black," he huffed. "No siree."

He sat up and sipped his bottle. The rain poured off the roof in torrents and in the cacophony around him, it seemed the only calming thing. He stood and removed his wool cap, twisting it in both hands to dry it a bit. He slid it into his coat pocket, knocking a knuckle against the short truncheon he fashioned out of an ash tree branch. He wrung out the bottom of his coat, but shot up as he did. He felt something was watching him. He looked out into the darkness, scanning the terrain by lightning. Once focused on a certain spot, Bill saw a shadow, a movement, in his peripheral and tried to catch it; each time he was greeted by more darkness. "You been following me?" he asked the storm. "Been with me since the road! I felt it!" he yelled and pulled out his club. "Well, come on out!" he said, waving his club in slow strokes. "I'm Bill Black! The meanest son of a bitch you'll ever meet! And I'm looking to put blood on my club!" he screamed.

Bill slowly backed into the house, his eyes going to the hill country around him. Once firmly in, he pressed against the wall beside the door and waited. He tried to sense the world with all his body, feeling everything and focusing on nothing. The rain collected in loud slaps. Thunder. He waited for footsteps. The sound of boots being pulled out of the mud. Anything.

Nothing.

He breathed easier for a moment. "Playing tricks on yourself," he said and gently rapped his cudgel against his shoulder. The house looked as though a wealthy rancher had lived and died there a hundred years ago. Bill knew he'd slept in worse places. A creak resounded through the walls, and he spun searching for it. He laughed at himself when he turned up with nothing.

"A fire," he whispered. "That's what you need, my boy."

He looked around the large room for anything to use as kindling. He took an overturned chair from beside a rat-eaten couch and broke it into thin pieces. At first, he looked at the couch the same as a waterbed, but a flash of lightning showed tiny stains of piss and flecks of rat shit. He scoffed and tore strips of upholstery off the couch and piled it on the remains of the chair. He went further into the house and noted the huge windows looking out into the rain. Some of the small panes were broken and cracked and an eerie moan seeped through them. A whisper in a language he couldn't understand.

Bill went into the kitchen and took wooden spoons and salad forks in one hand. The drawers of the island stove were empty, save for a rat carcass. At the back end of the house was a staircase. The center of it was caved in and the large hole in the ceiling was evidence enough of how. There were rooms on the floor above him and he stared at them until the lightning showed him their details. He only saw the tops of open doors and peeling wallpaper. He took the driest planks and parts of the banister back to the large living room, stopping at the kitchen to look over both his shoulders. There was a chill of spying eyes on the back of his neck. Reluctantly, Bill Black shrugged it off and arranged his pilfered kindling in front of a wobbly chair.

He patted himself and found his matches. The book was wet, but there were a few dry enough to use. He laid a flowery strip of upholstery across his knee and struck the first match. The drafty house quelled the meager flame with a single breath, but in the instant of dull light, he caught sight of eyes peering in through the front window. He shot out of his chair and took a spare leg in one hand and his club in the other.

He ran onto the porch swinging. There was nothing but the sound of rain. "Ah," he sighed, "if they could see me now. Jumping at nothing."

Bill went back to his woodpile and, shielding his final match like a rescued baby bird, he managed to set the old upholstery on fire. He quickly threw the foul smelling rag onto the old wood and got a good fire going.

He finished the rest of his bottle too quick for his liking and threw the container at the furthest wall. The tiny fragments of glass glittered in the fire light and Bill lost himself in the dancing colors. An Aurora Borealis in miniature. The light bounced and fluttered, causing the windows to look as though they warped and bubbled at their centers. Bill could not determine if the eyes were behind the glass or in front of it.

"There you are," he growled and threw a broken chair leg. It clunked beneath the window, but the eyes did not move. He pointed his club at the pair of unblinking eyes and shouted, "Don't you know who I am? I'm Bill Black! The meanest son of a bitch in Texas. I've killed sheriffs and deputies and took their wives right out their beds! I killed an old wolf with my teeth and beat a drunk Apache in a knife fight! And you don't scare me!"

The eyes did not blink.

"Now, you stop hiding and get what's coming to you," he chided and motioned the eyes forward.

A bolt of lightning lit up his view, stopping Bill dead.

There was nothing behind the eyes. Just the air and rain. They seemed to focus purely on Bill, who trembled. The boasts he'd roared for years seemed weak compared to those disembodied eyes. He and the window locked stares and the tinge of golden yellow around the ghostly eyes spun in slow revolutions. As they spun, the room filled with creaks of glass forming and reforming.

Like spreading veins, the disembodied eyes sprouted others in the panes around it. It was the newly grown pairs that set him back a step. He recognized them. The brown centers of his wife's eyes that bled down the walls to the three sets of eyes of the sons he'd never cared enough to see. Beside them, the muted greens of his mother and pale blue of his father glared down at him alongside the eyes of the old woman he maimed in Fort Worth. The nine sets from his old cell block girlfriends sent shivers down his spine that doubled from the sight of the fake purple eyes of the stripper he robbed in Archer City. "Get away from me!" he shouted at the watching windows.

In response, a bolt fell from the sky, drawing his panicked eyes up to the second floor. The doors were closed and against the lit sky, a great shadow of a goat or man or both loomed over him beside a nine-tailed wolf that stood as men do.

Bill Black had no boasts for them. The way Bill ran through the house, past the following eyes and the smoldering fire, it was as if he'd been running all his life. He ran as though it were his nature.

The house stood silently watching and was amused when the screams of Bill Black, the meanest son of a bitch in Texas, were louder than the thunderous night.

MARIO E. MARTÍNEZ

LUCKY FAMILY OF THE DECADE

I grabbed the hotel's door knob. "Come on, Stevey!" I said, opening the door.

"Dave, what happened to Mom and Dad?" My little brother turned to me, his eyes full of sadness. "I miss them."

I looked away, "They're gone," I sighed and walked inside quickly. I rang the bell of the concierge. A man, seeming to come out of nowhere, stood in front of me at the reception desk.

"Yes? What would you need, my good man?" He smiled a big, freaky smile.

"Yeah, uh, we need a room," I said, pulling out my dad's wallet from my pocket.

"Seventy-four dollars, please," he said, still smiling. I pulled out $75. I glanced about: it was really quiet and I didn't see a soul.

"Hey, where is everyone?" I asked, still looking around.

"They're all...gone," he replied, eye twitching. Then he muttered something unintelligible.

"Anyway, what's our room number?" I said, changing the subject.

"Dave, I'm hungry," Stevey complained.

I smiled and rustled his bright blond hair. "We have some tacos in Dad's car."

"Room 6C," the concierge interrupted, handing me the keys. He grinned. "Enjoy! I hope you never want to leave."

"Ooookaaayy. Well, Stevey, go to the room while I get the tacos, okay?" I handed him the keys. He nodded and quickly walked down the hallway.

"Oh, sir?" the concierge said, startling me. I turned slowly. "Are you 18 or older?"

"Oh, yeah. I'm 18," I replied, opening the front door. "I'll be right back."

AS I OPENED the car's back door, I wondered. *When am I going to tell Stevey about what happened to Mom and Dad? How do I explain who did it?* I wished I never had to tell him. I sighed and shook my head as if trying to shudder the memories away. I grabbed the bag of tacos and went inside.

I walked down the hallway and knocked on the door to our room.

"Stevey, it's me. I brought the tacos, and guess what? They're still kind of warm!" I said with forced enthusiasm. I heard slow, steady footsteps approaching the door, which then swung open. There stood Stevey, holding a remote. "Dave, there's a TV in here!" he said, smiling. "I thought three- or two-star hotels didn't have TVs!"

It was so good to see him smile. "First you need to eat, okay?" I instructed with a smile. "Come on."

WHEN WE WERE about finished, I noticed a weird gray substance on the wall about the size of Stevey's fists. *What is that?* I wondered, getting up and walking over to it.

"Stevey, go stay in the bathroom. This might be dangerous."

"Okay," he said, running to the bathroom. I realized that I had the salt container in my hand. *I should put this down.* I turned around quickly, causing some salt to fly into the air and land on the strange gray liquid on the wall. Out of nowhere, the liquid *screamed*. I fell backwards and saw the liquid shrivel up and darken.

"Dave, help!" Stevey yelled. I ran to the bathroom and opened the door: there was Stevey, standing on his tiptoes in the center of the room, grey goop closing in on him.

"Stevey, stay still!" I told him, running to the table. I picked up the salt container and hurried back. Then I started shaking salt all over the bathroom until the goop had completely shriveled up and darkened.

"Stevey, run over the goop! It's okay: it can't hurt you now."

He ran to me, obviously trying not to cry. "I'm scared, Dave," he whispered, clutching me.

"It's happening again, just like with Mom and Dad," I said, looking at the darkened goop. "Stevey, open the door."

I checked to see if there was more salt on the table. I found two packets and put them in my pocket.

"It's locked!" Stevey yelled. "The little lock thing was torn off, somehow! I swear it wasn't me," he added, twisting the door knob over and over again.

I ran to the door. Right next to it I saw some gray goop clinging to the wall with the lock mechanism sticking out of it. "Why is this happening again? I remember the goop that killed them!!!" I yelled at the oozing substance. "WHY?!?" I punched a hole in the door, startling Stevey.

"Dave, we should..." he whispered in a shaky voice, pointing to the goop coming out of the walls.

"Oh, crap!" I exclaimed, reaching my hand through the hole and unlocking the door with my key. Pushing the door open, I yelled, "Come on!"

AS SOON AS we started running down the hallway, the concierge appeared, goop far behind him cutting off our exit from the hall. The hotel employee frowned.

"Oh, you figured out his little weakness...salt." He started smiling again. "If any in your family happened to get this far, I thought it would be your father," he said, taking off his uniform and revealing a realtor's suit. Then he removed his wig and shook his long, real hair free.

"You," I whispered. Then anger swelled in me. "YOU SOLD US THE HOUSE! Then...THAT," I said, pointing behind him, "killed my parents." I took a deep breath and placed my hand on the wall. "Why us?"

"Dave...a VERY long time ago, I made a deal with a man, possibly a demon, for wealth and immortality...as long as I kill a family every decade, one that the goop monster chooses. And your family..." he grinned, "is the lucky winner of the decade!"

Suddenly the goop charged past him, rushing to kill us.

"Hold on, Stevey!" I ripped open the packets and threw salt on the floor, walls and ceiling, then finally on myself. There was no more then, so I turned to Stevey and shielded him with my body.

I WOKE UP surrounded by solid clumps of the goop monster. I crawled out from all the hardened mess, and then I remembered.

"STEVEY!" I screamed, jumping back in. I moved chunks of spongey nstiness around until I found him. I picked him up and laid him down on a flatter surface. I checked his breathing: no air.

No!" I started pounding on his chest and giving him CPR. No response. I kept pounding on his chest. "Come on, Stevey!" I repeated every time until I finally stopped and started crying.

I have to try one more time. I raised my fist in the air and slammed it down against his chest. Stevey suddenly opened his eyes and took a deep breath on awakening.

"Stevey?"

"Dave!"

I hugged him tight.

"Oh, okay, you're squishing me," Stevey gasped.

"Oh, sorry." I smiled.

I hadn't noticed the concierge sprawled in the middle of the solidified goop. He looked really old. He groaned:

"Dave, what have you done? Nooooo!"

Death interrupted him, and in an instant all that was left was dust and bone.

I turned to Stevey. "It's okay. He can't hurt us anymore. Now...let's find another hotel."

ANGELO BOWLES

ORPHIC EASTER EGG

Easter. Blake Garza had always hated Easter. The pain of hard eggs cracking against your head... Nope. Especially not with Max and his "homemade Easter eggs." So this time Blake went wandering in the "safe" forest.

"I don't think my parents will miss me, anyway." Blake sighed, leaning against a tree. He then slid to the ground and looked up at the sky... only to hear the crunching of leaves and feel an egg break against his head.

Of course, it was Maximiliano Sánchez.

"Okay, that is *it,* Max. I'm tired of your stupidity!" Blake yelled. Looking around for a rock or stick, he noticed an oddly colored egg lying nearby. He picked it up and threw it at Max. Max dodged the egg and ran off.

"See ya later, sucker!" Max yelled from afar.

Walking over to where the egg had hit the ground, Blake looked inside the broken shell. A shiny, bright, weird ball hovered up into the air.

I'd better call Cole! Blake, his hands shaking, pulled his phone from his pocket and dialed.

"Cole."

"Yes?"

"I found the weirdest egg, dude. It has a shiny, bright light floating out of it."

"Wait. What's the color of the egg?"

"Silver. I found it in the pine forest near my house."

"Oh my…"

"What? What is it?"

"Don't let it get its eggshell…"

"Too late! The light thing ate it or absorbed it or something. The shell just… kinda… flew into the light and disappeared."

"Okay, Blake. Stay where you are. I'm coming over."

Blake put his phone back in his pocket and poked at the light with a stick. The light devoured the stick and got bigger.

"I, uh, probably shouldn't do that," Blake whispered to himself.

"Step away from it!"

Blake turned around to see Cole Betancourt running toward him, his mop of black hair flopping against his glasses. When he was closer, Cole stared at the ball of light.

"Oh my God… it's the yolk of an Orphic Egg!"

Blake was confused. "The what of a what?"

"You never pay attention in class, dude. In the Greek religion these were known to hold the beginning of a new universe."

Blake was even more confused. "But… there already is a universe here…"

"Exactly. That's why our universe is probably… going to collapse."

"What?!? No! It can't. There has to be a way to stop this thing!"

"Um, not that I'm aware of," Cole said sympathetically.

Blake was freaking out. "What if we go back to where it came from?"

Cole shrugged and murmured something under his breath, but he agreed to go along with Blake.

"BLAKE, THIS IS POINTLESS. We're not going to find a solution. We have been scouring these woods for like four hours." Cole rubbed his eyes.

"Oh, OH, OK! Okay, yeah, let's just let the world END! Right! Hmm, yes, that's what everyone would do!" Blake yelled in a trembling voice. "Look! THAT STUPID BALL has gotten TEN TIMES BIGGER! It's got its *own gravitational pull,* Cole!"

Cole sighed. "Calm down. Just think: once this universe ends, there will..."

"NOPE!" Blake interrupted. "I'm not listening! Blah, blah, blah, NOPE!"

"You're really annoying. Instead of flipping out, you should understand that there will be a universe that's way better than this one."

Blake ignored him. "Let's keep looking."

AFTER ANOTHER FIFTEEN minutes or so, they came across a cave.

"Wait," Blake said. "What's this?"

Cole turned around. "Ah... Maybe your 'solution' is in here, Blake," he said, walking into the cave.

"I saw what you did with your hands there," Blake yelled after him. "You shut up!"

Inside the cave, the boys found all sorts of pictographs on the walls showing the ball and the egg.

"Whoa, looks like you were right, Blake," Cole whispered. "I think there's a solution nearby.

Blake looked at his friend. "Yeah. If we..."

He was interrupted by rumbling noises.

"Oh, no, Blake... We left the light by itself for too long!"

A large section of the roof of the cave shuddered and flew upward into the huge shining light that was the Orphic Egg yolk.

"Oh my God! A little *too* long!" said Blake in horror as the cave shook, sending pebbles raining down from the remaining roof. He opened his mouth to say something else, but a large rock smacked him in the head, knocking him into the dirt.

"BLAKE!" Cole yelled. Rushing to his friend's side, he checked his pulse. He was alive, but unconscious. "Okay, uh, I guess I'll pick you up." He hooked his forearms under Blake's arms and lifted, raising his friend partly from the ground. "Oh my God, you're heavy!"

Cole, stooped over, walked backward toward the entrance of the cave, half-dragging his friend. As if the cave didn't want them to leave, a huge part of the wall suddenly collapsed across the opening and pebbles rained down harder.

"Siiiiiiiiigggggggggggggghhhhhhhh..." Cole turned the other way. "Maybe there's another exit through here."

He made his way slowly toward the other end of the cave, avoiding rocks and stalactites. Finally he reached another chamber. Cracks forming in the roof allowed enough light in for him to see an altar standing before him, with two half-columns on either side. Atop each was a tiny bowl, one empty and the other containing an egg. An Orphic Egg.

Cole gasped. "This is the solution to our problem!" Excited, he let go of Blake without caution. His friend's head smacked against the cave floor, waking him up.

"What? What's..." Blake looked around. The giant ball of light was visible through the gaps in the roof. The entrance was blocked. Pebbles and dirt were beginning to stream toward the hovering yolk.

"HOLY SHIZZ!" Blake shouted as the gravitational pull of the baby universe grabbed him and started dragging him slowly. "Cole, how long was I KO'd?" he screamed above the rumbling roar.

Cole grabbed the second Orphic Egg and then caught ahold of Blake before he was sucked away. "I don't know... not that long!"

Blake's legs were yanked into the air, sending Cole off balance, slamming into the ground. He didn't let go of his friend though, and soon they were both being hauled through the air toward a huge hole. Blake was yanked through, but Cole braced one leg against the roof and clung to the other boy's jacket. He had a clear view of the ball of light, and it made him shake.

Small wonder. The Orphic Egg's yolk was as large as the local hospital.

Suddenly, the rock around the hole shifted, trapping one of Cole's legs. Screaming in pain, Cole let go of Blake, who went flying toward the light.

"Cole! What do I do?!?"

"Catch!" Cole threw the other egg at him. Blake caught it, barely. "When you get closer, throw it at the ball of light!"

Blake twisted in the air, looking at the pulsing universe growing above him. "Okay," he whispered to no one, and cocked his arm, pretending Max was standing there with a smirk.

The small egg left his hand and spun through the air, crashing against the original. Another mini-universe was born, but now the two began consuming each other, the roar and light seeming to blot out the world before they cancelled each other out and exploded.

A WHITE, HAZY LIGHT covered the land. Blake regained consciousness on top of what had once been the hill containing the cave. He sat up, his body bruised and aching.

"Cole?" Blake said. "COLE!!!"

He began pulling the rocks out of the way till he found his friend, hanging unconscious from the roof of the cavern. Pulling him up, Blake helped Cole free his leg. Hurt but smiling, the two stood slowly and looked around at the battered trees and setting sun.

Cole coughed. "Well, this is way better than the universe ending, I guess."

Blake nodded. "Yeah. I figure Easter's not too bad after all."

"Just be careful what eggs you pick up next time, dude."

THEY BOTH LAUGHED as the dust and smoke settled. The universe, of course, kept right on existing.

ANGELO BOWLES

LAS VOCES DEL LLANO

Welcome weary traveler, we are the spirits of the llano! In this secret place where two countries kiss we've made a permanent home. Where days have no number, the dead have no slumber, but still in the heat of day we take cover. The earth groans under the weight of this heavy sun, longing for water that may never come. Meanwhile the *chicharras* are singing in chorus calling for both rain and love.

You fell ill, amigo, and awoke from your fever with nothing but a small can of water and an old piece of paper as your means of salvation. El Coyote who betrayed us is back to his old evil tricks, but this time we won't allow him to win, so listen for us as we whisper the way on the cusp of these winds.

Abandonment stings your eyes, while the sun blisters your skin. Take your rest beneath the lone mesquite with its mangled body ever reaching towards Heaven. Bide your time, weary traveler: the sun will soon fade and a blanket of stars will then map out the way. Reaching into your pocket you pull out a photograph. Your beloved—she awaits anxiously for news of your safe arrival. "¡Por ti viviré!" you declare adamantly through tears. The sun pushes down as dusk settles in, leaving every hue of pink and purple to fill the sky, just like the color of her favorite dress.

Staring up at the star filled sky, searching for the brightest of them all, the North that will now be the key to survival. Our sun-bleached bones now glow under the light of this full moon.

Bones that once had flesh, flesh that once held life, fell prey to the hunger of man's greed. Do not be afraid of our bones, they cannot hurt you. They only long to go home, to lie amongst loved ones. Instead they lay here scattered by dust bowls, the playthings of wild dogs and curious creatures. Young, old, beautiful—the llano does not discriminate.

The hours drag on, as your body fights every step, threatening to welcome the respite of death. Hunger burns in your belly bringing confusion to your mind, when out of the darkness above you hovers an enormous winged creature. It's the *lechuza* in search of a meal! Her thunderous wings break the silence as she swoops in for a tiny mouse peeking out from under the ground. Hurry, follow our lead as I ride on her wings to the nearest road, for everyone knows she makes her nest on the telephone poles! Heart racing with hope, feet pounding the ground you give chase amongst the tall grass. Beware of the rattlesnake: her *cascabel* shakes and makes me want to dance! One of us will live, one of us will go on: it's enough to make this despondent spirit soar!

At last we've reached her destination. A broken-down pole along the side of an old country road where she feeds her young, proof that even in the most desolate place life does go on. Civilization is just a few miles down this not-so-traveled road where our journey together now ends. Remember us as you labor, remember us as you rest. The spirits of the llano wish you the very best!

EVANGELINA AYON

SUNSETS

I stand at the door way watching him, how did it get to this point? He was so strong and heroic in my eyes, he was my protector and best friend. I could lean on him knowing he would never let me fall; he was such a good person.

I looked around the pale white room; on one side was his bed next to the picture window, with a wooden chair next to it, the other half of the room was a mess. Papers scattered everywhere, pillows and blankets thrown, two hospital bags packed and ready, and folder with everything and anything you needed to know sat idle in the corner.

I take a breath and step into his room, its freezing but he doesn't complain. I stand over him watching him sleep in his bed, as I study this man's face. Who are you? I see the wrinkles lining his face, some are worry, some are the struggle, and others are laugh lines that never went away. His long eyelashes are bunched together, and his small lips lightly parted breathing evenly. He has this look on his face, disappointment, fear, pain I couldn't tell. I kiss his forehead, trying to let him know I'm here with him. Nothing changes. He doesn't even stir.

How did it get to this point? I feel a tear roll down my cheek; I raise my hand to brush it off, not realizing I was crying. I still remember the day that changed everything, Alzheimer's they said to me, what the hell is that? They give me all these pamphlets saying it'll explain everything in there; I knew it was bad if they didn't explain it face to face, I learned that quickly.

After going through them all I realized what it meant, it meant it he was leaning on me now. I would have to be the positive one for us both; I would be the strong and heroic one.

I sit by his bed just watching him, wondering if he will remember me when he wakes up or if I'm just another random person trying to help. The light in the room changes and I pull the curtain back, to watch the sunset, we did this every day, watch the sun go down and watch the world change right before our eyes. I pull my chair closer to his bed and reach for his hand; I look out the large picture window on the opposite side of his bed. A tear escapes again but this time I let it fall, it splashes on our hands and his eyes spring open.

I let out a chuckle and stand to look in his eyes, hoping for the best. "Hi." I smile down at him, he looks right into my eyes, but his face is blank, I don't give up. "You're just in time for the sunset" I say gesturing toward the window, he turns his head to look out the window. After a few seconds he looks back at me, like he's lost, he has that look on his face again I can't read it. "Soy tu esposa, Theresa." He shakes his head; he can't hear me, before I can tell him who I am again he turns his head back to the window. He doesn't turn back, I just let it go for now, trying to let him enjoy the rest of the sunset. Right before the sun hides away he turns back to me and looks right in my eyes I don't say anything.

We stare at each other for a while and he finally moves, he takes our intertwined hands and slowly brings them up to his lips and plants a soft kiss on my hand. He knows. He knows it's me, he knows I'm here, he knows I love him. I smile and kiss him on the forehead. "Te quiero mucho," I whisper and lay my head next to his; he puts our hands over his heart and nods his head. We stay frozen in this moment for minutes, hours, I'm not sure but I don't want to let go just yet. I hear him taking longer, deeper breaths knowing he fell asleep; I pull the covers over him and sit studying his face again.

This time I don't need to ask who this person is, I know. This man is my husband: I can see the wrinkles that line his face. Some are from winking at me too much, some are that silly face he used to make, some are from puckering his lips too much and some are laugh lines that never left his face. His long eyelashes are bunched together, and his small lips parted breathing evenly. He has this look on his face, peace, happiness, love. I can see it all, I kiss his forehead to let him know I'm still here with him, and his face stretches into a smile.

TIFFANY CANO

THE LITTLE GIRL

We sit at the table staring each other down, neither of us wanting to look away. I think back to the first time I saw her. I was leaving Mexico, my family, and my home. It was late at night when the pickup truck finally came for me.

"The first thing you do is get married!" I heard my mother yell over the noisy truck. I was eighteen and still had not gotten married. The solution: ship me off to Texas. My mission: get married. It was so dark outside that I couldn't tell if my mother was crying or not.

When I hopped into the back of the pickup was the first time I saw the girl. She was standing next to my mother, wearing a light blue dress with stains on it. She didn't have any shoes on, her hair was in knots, and she needed a bath. The girl looked like she was transparent and glowing; she had a sly smile on her face as if to say this was a stupid idea.

"Just leave him already, *mujer*!" she threw her hands up and rolled her eyes. I narrowed my eyes at her.

"That's enough out of you," I shot back.

Her eyes opened wide and she threw her head back laughing. "Listen to you, *mujer*, you sound like one of them."

I got up and decided to walk away from her; maybe she would catch a hint. She threw a plate at me, it hit the wall and shattered, I spun around enraged.

"*¡Te estoy hablando!*" she yelled. "Look at you, *mujer*, you don't look like yourself," she said, almost hurt.

I looked into the window reflection and studied the girl who looked back. She was blonde with her hair swept to the side, face caked with makeup. Contacts hid her brown eyes and changed them to a blue. She raised her hand to her face and saw her bright pink nails and enormous wedding ring.

The girl was right: she didn't recognize this person, this wasn't her. She had long black hair and was naturally beautiful. So why was she hiding behind all this? I turned to face the girl. She had a sly smile, "Go wash your face, *fea*," she winked; I smiled and ran to the bathroom to wash everything off. I sat and talked to the girl for hours and really started to feel like myself again.

"Sweetheart, I'm home! Who are you talking to?" He peeped his head in our bathroom and looked startled.

"*Hola, mi amor.* I was just talking to myself, I guess," I chuckled. I looked over at the little girl, and she was standing tall with her chest puffed out, proud.

His eyes opened wide in shock. "What happened to you?" he said, worried.

"*Nada, estoy bien,*" I answered back innocently.

The little girl whispered, "*Mujer*, he's talking about the way you look."

"Why are you talking like that?" he said, disgusted. "We talked about this. Get dressed, put your make up on and stop speaking in that Mexican gibberish!" He spoke through his teeth. "You are not allowed to speak, dress, or act like that here. Do you understand?" I looked up at him and nodded. "I'll be back in an hour. Throw the Mexican out and bring my wife back in, now!"

I sat on the floor for a few more minutes and finally looked up at the little girl. "*Vamos, mujer. ¡Está loco!*" she said, shaking her head. I watched her pacing the bathroom floor, talking about how we need to go back to México so we're safe. I was tired of her; she was always pushing to go back to México.

He wanted the Mexican out, so I needed to rid myself of my Mexican background. "Shut up, just shut up! I want you out!" She stopped pacing and stared down at me, "you don't know what you're saying, *mujer*. We need to stick together now more than ever. Get your stuff; *vamos a México.*"

I was upset but didn't understand why; I got up and pushed her with everything I had. She fell to the floor and looked scared. I barked at her. "No, I'm not going anywhere, listen and listen good. I want you out. Never show your face around here again, got it?" She stood up and shoved me until I was against the wall, "NO! *No voy a pedirte otra vez que cojas tus cosas*: let's go now!"

I was livid, I attacked her, and we fell to the floor forcing one another out. Everything went black, and the next thing I knew I was on top of the little girl.

"*Mujer*, don't do it! *Vamos a México*, we are safe there!" she struggled to get the words out.

"No! I live here now." I yelled and ended her.

AN HOUR LATER when he returned he saw his wife barely alive, thrown on the bathroom floor. She had a knife in her hand and was mumbling something. He rushed to her side, leaning his ear by her mouth.

"*Soy una mujer Mexicana.*"

TIFFANY CANO

NOBODY REMEMBERS DYING

I remember dying. It took place while I was living! I was out on a Saturday night just me and my girl, Amalia. We were having a "Saturday Night." Dressed to the nines I couldn't stop looking at her in her black ruffled dressed trimmed in red that ended a foot below her hips showing off all of her long legs made even sexier by those stilettos I bought her last Valentine's.

We had gone salsa dancing. ¡Ey, Ya Ya! We were getting all hot and heavy on that dance floor that night. *Picante*. She was kissing me on my neck. Nibbling on my ear. And I was moving to the rhythm. We were drinking tequila gold without the lime and salt and *echando gritos*. We had arrived at the club at nine and we didn't leave till last call. We left our car at the club and walked two blocks over to Rosita's Jalapeño Kitchen for some menudo to sober up before we made our drive home. Amalia and I were sipping our soup and talking about the older women with their *viejitos* out on the dance floor, laughing and saying how that would be us someday.

I heard Rosita in the kitchen. She sounded very upset. Rosita was a friend of my *tías* and I knew she had been having trouble with her son. I knew her son from high school. Even then, Michael had been trouble.

I heard a pot crash and a crack in the kitchen. It was followed by a horrific scream and cries. I rushed into the kitchen. Michael was there, and he looked like a mad man.

"I want money, bitch!"

Rosita was in the corner, her hands over her head for protection. Her face was red and covered with tears.

I turned towards Michael he pulled out a gun. I knew he was gone. Taken by drugs or alcohol. His eyes glazed over by a numbed pain. He aimed the gun at his mother. I rushed in front of her. He shot the gun 3 times. I remember his face, shocked at what he had done. I remember how he dropped the gun and ran. I remember the blood as it covered he floor and my clothes and Amalia's hands and beautiful raven hair as she wept over my dying body. And I remember her hiss that sent me silently into death.

ALYSSA AIDE VELA

LADY LECHUZA

The northern wind blew into the The Triple Kay ranch around dusk. I was a hand there the year I turned eighteen. I had worked on a ranch with my uncle in Starr County, in deep South Texas, since I was 12. He would pay me what he could. But he knew Mr. Kay would pay me well for packing hay that autumn and he recommended me to him.

"The harvest moon is aligned tonight," said Mr. Kay as we walked our way back to the ranch house, the cold wind cutting into our faces. We had worked till dusk and were now packing up for the day. I looked up to where he pointed. The full moon wore a reddish tint and was forming a triangle with two other stars. "Beware the Lechuza, Carlos", he said and he looked me in the eye. I chuckled. I had grown up hearing tales of witch owls. But I was no longer a child and there was no campfire in sight no reason to be telling me stories. "No laughing matter," he said sternly. "She comes by on fall days like these searching for her victims. The moon calls her out. A good looking kid like yourself oughta watch out. Best thing to do if you think you see her is go inside and shut the door. Or else she will be likely to suck your soul or gouge your eyes out."

(Listen to His story, listen to His lies)
(Escucha su historia, escucha sus mentiras)

"Yes, boss," I said just to appease him. As he headed to the barn I made my way to the covered patio. My boot went tap , tap, tap on the cement as I made my way to the backdoor where I knew there was a switch to turn on the patio lights. I put some extra nylon we had been using for the bales in a corner so we could continue to use it tomorrow and stood at the edge of the patio waiting for Mr. Kay to return.

Suddenly, white flashed in the night. I thought the moon had fallen out of its orbit and was chaotically falling to the earth. I step out from under the patio to see the night sky. The moon was nowhere in sight; it was hidden by the clouds.

(Sister Moon, bear witness to my sorrow; Sister Moon, do not forsake me)
(Hermana Luna, se testigo de mi tristeza, Hermana Luna, no me desampares)

Large white wings reaching 10 feet tip to tip were circling in the darkness. My eyes widened. Was it a ghost? Was it an angle? No, it was a giant white owl. "Lechuza," I whispered in the form of a breath that floated out of my mouth in a cloud of white that dissolved into the autumn night. The ten foot wings were fully expanded and were gliding to a landing. It landed about 50 yards away on a broad bough of a 300-year-old live oak tree whose arms wailed and raged at the starry sky.

(Ancient oak, my heart finds roots in your wildness; ancient oak, you allow me to approach while the crow and the raven will not come near me)
(Roble antiguo, mi corazón encuentra raíces en su estado salvaje, roble antiguo, permíteme acercar mientras la urraca y el cuervo no se acerquen)

I saw it perched on the branch, and I could not look away. It was only then that the wind blew and the moon showed her face as if she was too jealous to share the night sky with the great owl. As the moon light hit the ancient oak, the owl begins to transform. The great wings and snowy feathery coast vanished only to reveal silvery hair cascading over pale celestial skin. At first I thought this woman was as ancient as the oak she was perched upon.

(And I am as ancient as my sister moon; and I am as ancient as the script written on ancient tombs)
(Y yo soy tan antigua como mi hermana luna; y yo soy tan antigua como la escritura Escritas en tumbas antiguas)

The autumn air blew and her feathery strands floated into the chill air to reveal her cheeks. The marble-like flesh was smooth, not wrinkled. I did not know if she was good or evil. All I knew was that she was magical, and I wanted to be close to her. She sensed me. Slowly she looked over her right shoulder until her blue-grey eyes met mine.

(You who gaze upon me, do you dare to trespass on my solitude? You who gaze upon me, do you dare to tempt me with your youth?)
(Tú que me mira, ¿te atreves a traspasar en mi soledad? Tú que me miras, ¿te atreves a tentar con tu juventud?)

Her stare was piercing. She put her lips together and blew a deep, hollow whistle that filled the night. Uncontrollably I whistled back. In one swoop she jumped ten feet from the bough on to the ground landing on her bare feet. She turned around to reveal a supple thin frame. Her naked body was slightly plump at her hips, her thighs, her abdomen and her breast. She was a specter, white except for the subtle shades of pink at her cheeks, her lip and her nipples. And she was beautiful. Bewitchingly beautiful. Irrationally beautiful. Upon seeing her, knowing her, I left the confines of all logic. "Go inside," the voice of Mr. Kay rattled through my brain. Yet I stayed.

*(Tell me why you like my face, tell me why you like my fig-
ure, tell me why you do not look away)*
*(Dime por qué te gusta mi cara, dime por qué te gusta mi
figura, dime por qué no desvías la vista)*

Tap, tap...slowly my boots left the boundaries of the patio
and I approached her. In the time it took me to slowly walk less
than five steps she had transverse the field between up and was
standing feet away from me.

(And will you love me? And will you hold me?)
(¿Y me vas a amar? ¿Y me vas a abrazar?)

Her face was angular and angelic. Her curves were gravitat-
ing. Slowly we walked toward each other until we were inches
away. My body shivered from her energy. I exhaled another
cloud of steamy breath into the cold night. She said nothing but
her eyes marveled at my face. She raised her hand and ran her
fingers through my hair. Her fingers were cold to the touch. I
leaned in and gave her a soft kiss on the lips and pulled away to
gage her reaction. She answered with a passionate kiss entan-
gling us in a lovers embrace. I slid my hands over the curve of
her buttocks. Grabbed at her thighs and cupped her breast. She
had unbuttoned my shirt and threw it to the floor.

*(Are the stars watching us? Is the moon watching us? Who
is bearing witness?)*
*(¿Las estrellas nos miran? ¿La luna nos está mirando?
¿Quién es testigo?)*

Slam went the screen door, but, captured in her enchant-
ment, I would not hear it. Tap, tap, tap went Mr. Kay's worn-out
boots. Tap, tap...he left the concrete and hit caliche. I did not
feel him standing at my back. Click-cock went the shotgun. The

shell now rested in the barrel of the 12-gauge. Awakened by the sound of the weapon, I turned, leaving the lady exposed. Bang went the bullet into her chest.

(And he will stop my heart; and now he will end my story)
(Y ahora él va a detener mi corazón, ahora él va a terminar mi historia)

Now, a shriek erupted from the lady that pierced the ears of anyone around. This shriek simmered down to a continuous siren-like hiss. Clink-clank fell the gun on the on the rocky dirt just before the gunman's knees hit the ground. Grabbing his ears, he struggled to keep out the noise. I grabbed the lady. I wanted to protect her. I wanted to pacify her.

(You who love me want to cage me; you who love me refuse to let me alter)
(Tú, que me amas me enjaulas; tú que me amas no me dejas cambiar)

But her arms flailed back in fright. Her fingers turned into to feathers; her arm transformed into wings. I looked into her face, trying to calm her and reassure her that I was there for her. But only panic stared back at me. Then the beautiful, graceful face rounded, her eyes widened, darkened and sunk. They were now hollow holes of darkness. The lips I was kissing became now a beak that would not cease its hissing. I was still embracing her. I now realized I was no longer holding a lady, but an owl—an owl desperate to break free. An owl whose blood was dripping all over me. I loosened my grip. She started to fly. I panicked and tightened my arms. Her large talons clung to my torso, digging deep. They penetrated my flesh, my bones, my lungs, my heart. The moon hid behind another cloud as if to shelter itself from this catastrophe. Our blood was now joined in pools resting on the dry, dry South Texas earth as blood seeped out of our wounds and slid from our bodies.

(Now we are one; now we are none)
(Ahora somos uno; ahora somos ninguno)

Her massive wings flap. I know she wants to escape, but do not know if she wants to take me with her or if my weight is holding her back. The beating of her wings weakens. The blood loss is too much. The hissing stops. She releases her talons and falls to the floor. I fall on top of her. To my surprise I am in the arms of a Lady. Silence. Our eyes meet. I reach for her hand. I am with her as she gasps her last breath.

(I wished on the moon for something I never knew; I wished on the moon for...)
(Le pedí a la Luna algo que yo nunca conocí, le pedí a la Luna...)

Mr. Kay, now mobile again, released from the hissing, runs over to me and kneels at my side. "Son I warned ya," he reprimands as I am dying. My fingers had not yet loosened from hers. I held them tighter as I caught the eye of the moon that was now visible again. Then I let go.

ALYSSA AIDE VELA

LAS LECHUZAS DE FALFURRIAS

L egend has it that the lechuzas of the Texas-Mexico border have relocated to the town of Falfurrias, Texas. Although the breed has diminished to a few, their reputation is still well known.

Unlike their counterparts of old, the lechuzas have not died out and are promised to return to great power. It isn't common sense why the lechuzas were isolated to make their home in this town, but it is rumored that the collapse of the Reynosa Bridge in 1934 had an impact on the decision.

Intuition tells me that they have intentionally been keeping a low profile, only I can't figure out why. They are born as women, but when their powers are unlocked, they have the ability to transform into owls.

Though they are viewed as witches that work only with black magic and bad intentions, this is not actually the case. They are half human and half witch, a characteristic most of us share. They mostly have good intentions but could be trapped with the moods of greed, lust, and hate. These are the cases in which their power turns sour, the ones remembered by history.

The lechuzas shouldn't be cursed for preferring to work with black magic against the white magic of nature. They weren't born with the power of both. The white magic they know has survived in them from the teachings of the Mariposas.

Do not blame them if their craft wreaks consequences on others. You don't know what it is like living with powers that are discriminated against but hypocritically called upon by commoners that don't let the charms die out. Lechuzas have stronger feelings than you or I.

Don't bother them with foolish requests. They can abuse their powers to keep you from annoying them. Trust me, this is not done in a nice manner...

It can't be known what particular lechuza will answer your call. Remember, each has a different personality and intention. They are our sisters and mothers, aunts and neighbors. So call only when it is truly a great need.

To call them out, you have to speak in a firm and demanding, but sincere voice. Use a rope made out of horse tail and tie seven knots that are less than an inch apart. While doing so, recite the following chant after making each knot:

> *"Woman of disguise,*
> *lady of dark charm.*
> *sister of white light,*
> *listen to my call;*
> *come fly in soft hue flight,*
> *I do not fear you,*
> *craft of blood in me,*
> *listen to my call."*

Then you'll need to repeat the process, but backwards. Do so by saying the chant before untying each knot. Please do not make a mistake in this process of calling them out to you because you might accidentally hypnotize them, and they will hurt you instead.

If you are successful in calling them out, do not be fearful—do not risk offending them.

I am sure that sometimes, at night, you can hear them scratching your roof. Do not shoo them away because they need to take breaks between long flights. And they may just be carrying a good omen for you.

PRISCILLA CELINA SUÁREZ

WHAT I KNOW OF MARIPOSAS

For some five years now, I've been researching the myth of the Mariposas. I learned of their existence from my great-grandmother Antonia De La Garza, who died a few years back in San Juan, Texas. Of all the people I have asked, only one woman other than my abuela has validated this myth.

This woman agitated about the end of the Mariposas, their duties on earth, and her own theory of why that myth has disappeared from our folklore. Her name, though, I am obliged to keep secret, and much of her information is too personal to disclose.

Of all the sources I've studied, there is little or nothing to mention about this particular breed of white witches. At random times, I wonder if their story was all made up. But then I listen to other narratives of shamans and curanderos—men given the power to heal people. Their powers are so similar to that of the Mariposas. Maybe their associations resulted in drastic consequences and are not remembered because of the discreetness of these women towards past provisions.

What I can tell you about these ladies is that they were once the sisters of lechuzas. But that was long ago. They inhabited the land in their sisters' shadow, cautious and discreet regarding their powers. Yet people's natural instincts tend to anticipate who is enchanted with supernatural forces. One can always see the fear of the eye.

Same as their sisters, the white ladies were born into handsome bodies, wearing their hair well below the waist.

They were born into the line of their female descendants. Mariposas were one-third human, one-third witch, one-third glorified. They lived as women did, but each was capable of turning into a butterfly resembling the breed of monarchs. That is, if the girl accepted to be baptized into her powers. Once she did, her charms bloomed with practice.

Until the girl accepted her path into this lifestyle, and her powers had been granted, she was free of duty. She had the choice to chose her endowments or continue living a normal existence. Mariposas had a huge role to play. They were the angels that people unknowingly prayed to, the ones in charge of completing reasonable grants. Because of the duties bestowed upon these ladies, few of them actually married and had children.

Humans feared their qualities because we have trouble accepting what we don't understand. It is for this reason they were associated with lechuzas. Not that their sisters were bad women. They simply had been dispensed a bad reputation.

I wish I had more to tell you about these marvelous beings, but the truth is that sources have run dry on this topic.

I doubt that their entire blood line has become extinct. For this reason I affirm that many females from south Texas have a chance of being a descendant or being related to one. If that is so, all that you need to do is accept the duty as a Mariposa and you will be honored with the charm. But do so only if you are prepared for the responsibility that will be granted with it.

PRISCILLA CELINA SUÁREZ

MISSED CONNECTION

Ryan built the machine that would take him back to when she was still on Earth. He had his final will notarized. Research papers, prototypes and instructions concerning the Device were passed on to curious colleagues.

Frank called and left a frantic message: "They found Sarah! She's back! The Greys returned her!"

Ryan never heard the message; his cell was accidentally transported during a preliminary test.

Life on Planet Keeps would be permanent. Sealed in a space suit, Ryan boarded the Device.

Among those in attendance at Ryan's Memorial service was Sarah. She had purchased the biggest flower arrangement.

ANNA SOLÍS

LITTLE TICKLE

11:15 a.m.

At five, she knew there was great difference between the good and sweet old princesses and the dark, callous villains. It was not normal to like Maleficent and Ursula compared to Aurora and Belle (at least for someone her age). To keep that fact a secret she lied about who her favorite characters were, easily pulling off the facade due to her liking the color pink.

Left pinky down.

At the age of six, the child accidentally dissected a caterpillar. She really didn't mean to. She merely wanted to help it speed along on its path of life by removing the green ooze that gushed out of its middle. When it slowed to the point of lying still, she thought it was waiting for her to remove more of the gunk.

Left ring finger down.

She knew it was weird to enjoy reading the Fear Street series as a seven-year-old. She hardly understood the books, but she found the main antagonists fascinating. The Goosebumps novels were still interesting, but they had no details of corpses and warped human mentality that made her spine tingle in something she at the time learned was called excitement.

Left middle finger down.

Her understanding of death was nearly complete when she was eight. She was running in the school's dirt track for Phys Ed. when she saw a crow lying in the middle of the path. Mud was already clumped within its feathers and around the open eyes, but nevertheless she picked it up and lovingly carried it. Half an hour later, the teacher saw what she was doing and told her to leave the bird then wash her hands.

Left index finger down.

Weeks before she reached the age of eleven, the girl always wanted something to be off about her. When she first saw the film *The Sixth Sense* in the seventh grade, she thought the answer to being different from most humans lied in seeing the dead. Ghosts and things of the sort were subjects science failed to explain—it was magic at its best, no matter how wrong and shadowy it seemed. Plus, having a well-developed sixth sense would help her self-isolation. In every story there was someone who preferred being alone; she wanted to try that.

Left thumb down.

She was twelve when she read her first Edgar Allan Poe story: "The Tell-Tale Heart." It was an intriguing tale of insanity—her very first step into the genre of Gothic horror. Her second Poe short story was an assigned reading in her first year of the high school: "The Cask of Amontillado." It was another enthralling trip of possible lunacy, and when she reached the end of the tale she discovered she wanted to write messed up shit just like that—she wanted to create that sort of utter perfection, the way Alice had created her own Wonderland.

A left hand and right thumb were now outstretched over her open notebook. The owner jerked her head up and glanced around at her classmates, imagining her younger self walking past the desks and studying each and every one of them, deciding who would be it. Her present self twitched her fingers when the apparition paused in front of the teacher, gazing up at the adult with large, twinkling eyes. They both wondered how it would feel to shave off the person's skin before the real one quietly sighed and jotted down another note, glancing at the electric clock to her left.

11:17 a.m.

Only two minutes have passed since she began to analyze herself again.

She faced the front again, where the child version of herself looked back expectantly and twiddled her fingers towards her as if to cast a curse. She imagined those fingers shoving themselves through the larynx of the student to her right (since they were closest and therefore easiest to picture manipulating their anatomy) and placed herself in their shoes. The ghost sensation of something piercing her neck caused her to shudder self-consciously. She would definitely be too sensitive and ticklish to the touch. Then she placed herself in the imaginary body of her past self, where those digits burrowing through fresh flesh would be hers. The sensation of wet meat surrounded them and pressed underneath her gnawed fingernails... Oddly, the unreal scent of copper made her mouth water and she wanted to lean in for a lick, wondering if that was what Andrei Chikatilo felt whenever he killed.

The teacher called her attention, and she smiled sweetly at the world.

11:18 a.m.

MAGALY GARCÍA

JJ AND THE CUCUY

JJ was a scrawny little boy born and raised in Mission, Texas, a small dusty border town at the edge of the known world. As Rio Grande Valley tradition would have it, being the first born male, he was named after his father, making him Juan Joel Medrano, Jr. It was not only the fact that JJ was born in this tiny border town that made him peculiar. JJ was also born and raised as a Testigo de Jehová or Jehovah's Witness. His dad had been raised as one and his father before him. It was the only life JJ had ever known.

His mother, on the other hand, was the only member of her family that converted from their strong Baptist roots to become a Jehovah's Witness, and she was content to live out her days, and raise her sons in what they lovingly refer to as "the truth". Now, being raised as a witness wasn't really any different than being raised in any other house, with one exception. In JJ's home, there was no Santa Claus, no Easter bunny, no tooth fairy, and no great pumpkin. Those things were a lie and JJ's parents explained that they would never lie to him. So JJ grew up knowing that the adults in his life would never tell him anything that wasn't the absolute truth.

JJ was ten upon the arrival of his little brother Eric into the world. A ten-year-old on summer vacation, a new born baby, a husband at work all day, and the scorching South Texas June heat—it was almost too much for JJ's mother Elva to handle. It was then decided that JJ would spend a week or two with Elva's family on their ranch in Alice. JJ was excited and happy to go, especially since it meant leaving behind that smelly creature that had taken over his room, his life, and his parents. Certainly he would find a sympathetic ear in Alice.

The ranch in Alice was not really an ranch at all, but a colonia of trailer lots, neatly lined up one after the other, all purchased by the sweat and blood of abuelo Pacheco, one for each of his five daughters and two sons. When you pull into the colonia, the first house on the left belongs to abuela. It had once been a beautiful house with a clean cut yard, but since abuelo had died, the grass had taken over, and the house was slowing falling to pieces. Across from abuela's house in this cul de sac of Pacheco's was tio Veve and next to him, tio Sammy. Next to abuela's house was Tia Julie's lot, but since she stayed with abuela and never put a trailer on it, Veve used it to house his *gallos*.

Next to that stood Elva's empty overgrown lot. She had always wanted to put a house on the land her papi gave her, but after she married Juan, he quickly moved her to the RGV to be with his family. "One day, *hijo*, this will be yours." JJ stood in the middle of a dilapidated lot with grass up to his waist, a lot of gallos to his left, and his tia Adele's broken down trailer to the right. He decided right then and there that Eric could have it.

Tia Adele's house was the worst, but it wasn't her fault. She had three rambunctious boys and all of the latest movies and video games. With Sammy's boys living within walking distance and all their friends not far off, her house didn't stand a chance. If it could be jumped on, swung on, or wrestled over, it was.

The last house that centered the colonia was Tia Cuca. She was the social butterfly of the colonia and of Alice. She was strict and had no patience for roughhousing. She was short and perfectly round, but when she was mad, even tio Veve was scared of her and he was at least a foot taller and as strong as an ox. When the boys got too loud she would yell at them to go outside if they were going to act like animals and tio Veve would chime in,

"Andiamo, you better go! Your tia is crazy!" Then he would help himself to another piece of pan dulce from the table while she wasn't looking.

JJ began playing tag with his cousins running from house to house, while all his tios and tias drooled over the bald bundle sleeping in Elva's arms.

What was so special about him anyway? He couldn't even walk. Even abuela was sucked into his web.

Stupid baby.

AB tagged JJ and he took off after him. Young, free, and surround by family. Safe.

His parents strapped Eric into the car seat and set off on their journey back to the Valley. JJ and his cousins continued to run up and down the street playing Transformers, riding bikes, and seeing who was stronger or who jumped farther or climbed higher in the trees.

It got dark and a sweet summer breeze blew in the trees. AB's cheeks were red and his hair was matted from sweat. When he went into abuela's house to get a drink, all five of the boys followed. The tias were sitting with abuela in the living room watching a novela when the boys trampled in. Lining up for a drink of water soon became a laughing match and who could spit water. Cuca jumped up from her chair and ordered the boys out of the house and down to Adela's.

"And be quick about getting there before the Cucuy gets you," she added.

"The Cucuy?" JJ looked at Cuca, puzzled.

"Yes, the Cucuy! He comes and takes children away that are not behaving right."

The other boys filed out the door and you could hear them shouting and laughing all the way to Adele's house. JJ stood at the screen door looking out into this now unfamiliar darkness.

The Cucuy?

He stepped out onto the porch, his knees shaking. A gallo crowed. JJ bolted from the porch and ran, heart in his throat, to Adele's house. He sat in a corner of the living room the rest of the night—he would not be moved. The next day his parents were called and they made the two hour journey to pick him up.

NINA MEDRANO

HUEVOS A LA RANCHERA

S he places the plate in front of me, steaming hot with huevos a la mexicana, ranch style beans, and papas. A warmer with fresh tortillas de harina she places on the side. Steam from the coffee, sin crema y azúcar, rises and mixes with the incense from my altar breakfast plate.

I take my napkin and lay it across my lap. Pause. I know I should pray. Praying before I eat had become such a habit that when I reach straight for my fork, I feel awkward, like I've tripped over my shoelace on a busy street in front of a crowd of people who all stop and stare at me.

I know I should pray. I want to pray. But I am too smart to pray. I pick up the hot sauce and sprinkle it over the huevos.

Hail la Cholula, full of spice, save me from my sins.

I grab two aspirin from my purse, clothes still reeking of smoke and beer, and I take a bite. The jalapeños mix with the sauce and a fire ignites.

Hail la Cholula, full of spice, save me from my sins.

I feel it burn as it slides down my throat. I am on fire, but I do not flinch. I am used to it.

Hail la Cholula, full of spice, save me from my sins.

I know I should pray. But I can't. I am too smart to pray. *Y yo tengo huevos.*

NINA MEDRANO

TODO ESTÁ BIEN

The *cucuy* is real. I don't get why people ask if I believe in him. He looks like a golem—covered in fresh, caked mud. He doesn't walk; he crawls. If he walked, his knees would crack. He takes his fat hands and places them in front of him and pulls himself forward. This is the reason he hides under beds. You see, he can't get up any higher.

If he were to try to climb up on the bed it would take too long. The reason he comes out at night, is easy to explain—the lack of sun. The sun would dry him out and he would end up looking more like Lot's wife, a stiff pillar of salt rather than a creature from the netherworld charged with making children fall asleep on time or behave properly.

Duérmete, o si no, vas a ver—va venir el cucuy.

Does anyone know what he was supposed to do when he gets there? I just assumed he would touch my feet. That seemed creepy enough, since he would be cold. But, thinking about it in the daylight of adulthood, what was supposed to happen?

And the same can be asked about *la mano pachona*. How did it get so hairy? How did it become disembodied? So many questions.

But, these are the fantastical collective beliefs of my culture.

These creatures do not harm, not for real. Like all things in life, we can only truly be hurt by those closest to us. Just like a woman or husband is more likely to die at the hands of a spouse than a stranger.

Case in point, my dead grandmother came to see me in a dream in the winter of 2007. *Abue*, as I called her in my dream, died of emphysema when I was 5 years old in back in 1973. I only remember those things about her that I have been told. She was a three-pack a day smoker, and she loved my father over his sister.

In my dream, I carried a toddler. He was about 18 inches in height, with curly yellow locks, in a white Huggies diaper. He was sick, so much so he remained fast asleep while I walked out of the house for some reason.

It was then I noticed Abue in the middle of the yard.

"¿Qué pasa?" she asked. Now, I have to tell you that I do not dream in Spanish. My primary dream language is English, and that has only changed once in over 30 years, and that one time was this dream.

"Abue," I said. "El niño está enfermo."

She tightened her thin dry lips to form a tiny line across her lower face. Two crevices appeared just above her nose. She wore a white linen dress and a multi-colored scarf that draped over her shoulders. Her deep, brown, wavy hair draped at her neck.

"Dámelo," she ordered. I gave up the child. His eyes remained closed and the hair on his forehead was damp from perspiration. He remained unresponsive.

"Ru, ru, ru, ru," she sang while rocking him. "No te preocupes, ya estoy aquí," she said softly.

"Okay," was all I said.

By this time, her attention remained on him. She sat in the middle of the lawn.

"Ru, ru, ru, ru," the song continued.

By her feet, a tree burst from the ground. Before me it sprung vibrant green leaves leaves and white petal flowers that bloomed within minutes..

"Ya ves," she said. "Todo va a estar bien." She kept rocking.

I smiled. Things were going to work out. But, I wondered about his problem. It was then I looked down and realized the situation. His little thigh turned black, and while literally it was his thigh, the form I saw was undeniable—the shape of a liver.

"Oh, no. It's his liver," I said. That was his problem. She smiled at me rocking back and forth while she looked at the tree, she knew I understood.

"Va a estar bien todo," she repeated.

I woke up to find my mom and dad having coffee in the kitchen. I told them about the encounter. Creases between my father's eyes formed immediately. We came to the conclusion that the dream had to be about my nephew, Jake.

Earlier in his life, Jake had been diagnosed with fatty-liver disease, a result of too many McDonald's Happy Meals. We woke the poor kid up that morning and dragged him to the doctor. The blood work came out fine, still not to take any chances our diet immediately changed. Salads and baked items became the norm.

"Nomás era para darnos un susto," my mom proclaimed.

But, that wasn't the case.

In June of that year, my father handed me a paper full of columns and percentages he got from the doctor.

"No sé qué dice." His face was paler than normal. He understood.

Metastatic liver cancer.

No word, no cucuy or bruja inspired the helplessness I felt.

"It's the liver," I said. In a flash, I found myself in the backyard. My grandmother held her child in her arms.

"Todo va a estar bien," she rocked him gently back and forth beneath the tree.

Over the next five weeks, my dad withered in front of me.

How was anything ever going to be fine?

One day, he collapsed on his way to the bathroom. Six hours after he was admitted to the hospital, he passed away. For most of that time, he held his hands up praying, chanting, his face the most disjointed I had ever seen.

In the end, I begged the universe for relief. I wished each breath he took be his last, I prayed he die.

During his funeral, a life-long friend of his commented on how much Jake looked like Dad.

"No tienen porque están sufriendo. Allí lo tienen. Míralo, con todo y el pelo güero."

"Papi no tenía pelo güero," my sister corrected her.

"¿Nunca sabían? Sí, tu papi era bien rubio cuando era chiquillo."

In that instant, I understood fully.

Abue predicted the whole thing, my caring for Dad, and eventually her coming to take her favorite child home.

Todo estaba bien.

And that tingling in the back of my neck I get each time I think or tell this story is her, reminding me things are how they need to be.

MARIANITA ESCAMILLA

THE LIGHTNING STORM

We all wake and find out we are born into things we didn't desire. The sad truth is that some storms have gone on for years. We all are searching for shelter. Unfortunately, we become the newest casualties of someone else's vices and often plagued by a past not our own.

It is one of those rare summer mornings. Rain and strong winds bruise our Valley. Four students have arrived early and sit on a bench in the hallway, waiting for their classes to begin. The four are taking different classes. They don't know each other, yet they're familiar and have seen each other several times before. Mounted on the wall near the ceiling is a television monitor. The news is on and in a short segment the four learn of an attack on a convoy that has left seven Marines dead.

Among the group is a young woman who wears a new white petticoat and sits sipping coffee. The smell of the coffee is pleasant, a comfort amidst the unusual weather. She whispers, "I thought the war was over. Didn't the President say it was over?"

An older, but still young-looking woman sitting next to her, puts down a dark backpack that is full of books. Despite its weight, when she carries it she always stands straight. For her it's like lifting feathers. She answers, "The president before him said the same thing about the same war. I don't know for sure, but I think presidents live in dream worlds where wars end."

A boy in his late teens sits with his face buried in a book. Lifts his head and asks if anyone had served in the military and, joking, he asks if anyone had any advice that could ease the stress he was feeling about having to take a brutal mid-term. Later that day he would face the Grim Reaper, academically at last. The elder woman answered, "If the heat don't drive you insane, the professors will."

Chuckling a little the fourth person in our group speaks. "Near ten years ago I had finished Airborne training and was sent to Iraq. I was stationed in a remote and quiet place in Iraq, Intel suggested that the area was about to get heavy with action and my unit was placed there in case shit got out of hand, but nothing happened. Intel screws up a lot. Anyway, everywhere we went the people treated us like liberators, we would patrol the goddamn streets without worry."

"You were Airborne? Man that's awesome! And this other guy is nervous over some little exam. He and Petticoat were in junior high having easy lives while we were training to fight and die. You know I made history? I was one of the first women to be accepted to Ranger school and I would have finished too."

The young woman sees a few friends standing at the end of the hall. She gets up and goes to join them. Needing to study, the young man leaves and goes into an empty classroom where his class is soon to start.

Wondering about her experience at with the Rangers, he asks, "So what happened at Rangers, and why leave it undone?"

"The cycle was nearly over and graduation was only about two weeks away. I had been made squad leader and there was one guy...he didn't look like he was gonna make it, he started getting real quiet. Some of the instructors and I were watching him. We didn't know what might happen. It was like he was there but not, you know? His face was an empty stare. One night he was talking about how he hated everything and wanted out. I reported it but nothing was done, and the next night he made his break."

"You did right by telling your superiors. If they fail to act that's their fault. So, what happened next?"

"When he started going AWOL, I followed, so I could stop him. Caught up to him, told him not to go and that we all need to help each other, then he took a swing at me and I swung back. MPs showed up fast like from nowhere. Arrested me, and the guy give them the story that I was the one going AWOL, and that he was stopping me....the bastards believed him."

"That's not cool. So what did they do to you?"

"Some lieutenant said I had slept with him in order to get into Rangers. They also made up some bullshit charges against me. None of it was true, it was like they just wanted an excuse, and were waiting for me to screw up. I earned everything and was given nothing. Anyway, that ass got an accommodation from the goddamn captain and they gave me a dishonorable discharge."

"They probably just wanted you out. Like we can't have some girl kicking more ass than us dudes." With a smirk on his face he turns to her and says, "Forget the M16; you need to learn how to operate an oven. War is for the tough, women are weak. Go fix a pot roast, ha ha."

She laughs and punches him in the arm, "*Pinche* Airborne, so what about you: why did you get out?"

"Contract ran out. Before signing up I was married and had two baby girls. I needed to get back and be a father. They were riding in the back seat while their mother was driving to the airport to pick me up. A drunk, speeding through an intersection slammed into the side of the car. My wife made it out okay, but the girls didn't have a chance. We held the marriage together for a few years but we never got over the loss and drifted apart. Here, look I carry this with me everywhere." He shows her a picture of his daughters that he takes from his wallet.

She looks at it, "They were beautiful girls."

"Thanks, they were...they *are* beautiful girls."

"I'm sorry. If I had known, I wouldn't have asked why you left."

"It's fine: you had no way of knowing. Beside, you gave me your story. If you want to feel sorry for someone feel sorry for those dead Marines. You know that's where I should be. I should be out fighting alongside them. My girls would still be alive, if I had stayed."

"Yeah, I know what you mean by being out there with them; in some ways we never forget we're soldiers, in a way there's no such thing as ex-military. But hey! Don't blame yourself with things you can't control. It's all fate and chance, no one commands the future. It don't mean anything: it's all shit."

The two part, each wishing the other a good day, and both go to their classes.

Well into the night. Sitting alone with his memories and sorrows collected over the entirety of his life. The dawn is now greeting the Valley. His final words are to his inner demons. He speaks to them as someone speaks to old friends.

"Well time to make way for the young, the new, and let them grow without old bastards like me passing on bitterness. I'm tapping out; just want y'all to know that if there is an afterlife, I'll have my revenge by living without regret and y'all won't control me. I'll rise above fear and never fade into sadness and always act with courage and honor!"

He puts a gun to the side of his head, readies it. Takes a last breath, holds it for a second and releases. He closes his eyes and pulls the trigger, taking his own life.

Now lifeless, his body sits. For him the war is now over and only in his death is he finally at peace.

WILLIAM MAINOUS II

DRIVING THROUGH SPOTLIGHTS

Night sky stripped of moon and stars, replaced by gray clouds. The buildings vanished from my view, leaving a long road illuminated by street lamps, a frozen, black river up ahead. Realized that I ventured too far from the city, I decided to head back. I took a left and found a long, barren road with street lamps placed on each side, the very image of a hallway in a gothic manor. Even with Katy Perry on radio, nothing distracted me from the unsettling feeling of isolation, wishing for other cars to come driving by.

Looking ahead, I made out a group of small figures under the spotlight of a street lamp. I drove closer and saw children standing in a circle laughing at a girl with her mouth wide open and cheeks reddened and wet, clenching her stained skirt on her knees in a red puddle. Despite the soundproof windows, laughter and sobs echoed in my mind. I drove on and looked ahead turning the volume up.

I heard a loud bang to my right. My eyes turned to see a man lying in another spotlight. There were people walking across, unaware of the dead body on the ground, not even noticing the bloody footprints left behind. I kept driving, looking ahead and turning the volume up some more.

Farther down the road, I forcefully stepped on the brakes when my path was blocked by white men in business suits furiously stomping on the ground. A mouse was running around, tied to a small pole, escaping from giant soles. I honked at the men to get off the road, but they kept trying to kill the mouse without even flinching.

I could just run them over. No one would know nor give a damn, I thought, remembering the apathetic children and people walking by. *One hard step against the pedal, they'll be dead like old dogs.* Overwhelmed by my superego, I just drove around and took a left turn.

My apartment complex was up ahead, and I drove towards the parking lot. After getting out of my car, images still branded in my memory, my hands shook with fear, but mostly out of guilt and frustration. I went inside my apartment and locked the door. Took my pills before bed.

DIANA ELIZONDO

BEFORE I PAINT

My latest model had finally arrived. No appointment had been made, as was usual in these cases. Walking up the stairway, he came into light, letting me examine him from a distance. Young adult in early twenties, hair shoulder-length and shining gold. Quite built, but not too muscular for my standards.

He entered my office and poured himself some wine. Without my permission, of course, though I was never bothered by that manner. After finishing his wine, the model took few steps: slow, clumsy and shaky. I grabbed his shoulders to hold him still. Refusing my aid, he struggled out of my hands. Roughly pushing away, his foot slipped and he fell down the stairs.

I watched him tumbling to the tiled floor, hearing bones crack against the stairs like marionette limbs. Following down the stairway, eyes still locked on him, staring back at me without awareness. Looked more divine on flowing crimson beneath than white marble alone. I captured his beauty with a flash of my camera, anxious to begin painting.

DIANA ELIZONDO

AN ANGELENO'S ASSIMILATION

When I attempt to enlighten my friends, and a variety of business and government entities as to my present whereabouts in Harlingen, I often have to narrowly define the area as being located in south Texas near Brownsville—*not* the suburb of Dallas, "Arlington," that's home to NFL's Cowboys. That's "Harlingen" with an "H", although to this day, I'm not sure of the correct pronunciation of the city's name: is it HarlinJEN, or HarlinGEN?

Here are just a few observations this former Angeleno has about this municipality.

One of the biggest adjustments I've had to make is my ongoing efforts to adjust to the weather. It seems that summer here lasts year 'round, with what seems like an average temperature of 99 degrees, and 100% humidity. There's maybe a week or so in "winter" where sometimes the thermometer will drop to 50 degrees, and humidity goes down to 90%.

This is quite a change from Los Angeles, where area Chambers of Commerce like to boast of their year-round average temperature of 75 degrees. When it does warm up on occasion, it's a dry heat coming off the Mojave Desert. The word "humidity" is only alluded to during the intermittent rainy season.

Rush hour in Harlingen happens when you're 10 minutes late for an appointment "on the other side of town", and you get caught in traffic, waiting for a freight train to meander across the middle of the 2 major east-west arteries, Tyler and Harrison, respectively. This can happen at any time, on any day of the week. The actual schedule of the trains is a mystery, apparently known only by the conductor - and God.

On the other hand, traffic in LA is caused by (a) folks slowing down to take a picture on their cell phones of someone pulled over on the shoulder changing a tire, who vaguely resembles a celebrity, (b) a celebrity murder suspect trying to flee law enforcement in a slow-speed chase as onlookers shout "the Juice is Loose"; and (c) too many vehicles.

Folks here in south Texas mark the passage of time by the number of hurricanes they've been through, and, especially during the drought, reminisce about the rainfall that Alex and Dolly brought.

It's kind of the same thing with earthquakes in southern California. Bragging rights of a sort occur when you can pinpoint your "closeness" to the epicenter with the least amount of damage, not to mention survival—as in, "I was 3 miles from the Northridge quake, and all that happened was the water heater ripped from its mounting flooding the kitchen when it crashed to the floor—and my dog chased a wayward goose from the yard".

At least with a hurricane you can see the storm approaching on live Doppler radar. Unfortunately, there's no proven method of predicting earthquakes, unless you include a cat clawing an opening in the back of your sofa, refusing to come out of his refuge, as an indicator that a large phenomenon is about to transpire. In LA, you KNOW the "big one" can happen any day, but you can't seem to get around to stocking your emergency supplies. You go about your daily routine in denial - not just a river in Egypt, but a way of life in southern California.

The mountains in Texas are about 800 miles away in the western part of the state, and the horizontal landscape is broken only by emerging strip malls and palm trees. The tallest attribute that Harlingen can claim is any on-ramp to the expressway.

I do find myself longing for my southern California kitchen-window view of the snow-capped Sierra Nevadas—when I could see through the smog.

By the way, does burning sugarcane bother anyone besides me? The proximity of the smoldering fields seems to lie in direct correlation to the day I wash my car.

Local legislators and judges here in south Texas are some-how able to keep their government benefits despite their felony convictions. In California, there are also no apparent conse-quences that affect these benefits for former governors commit-ting adultery.

Finally, why is it that our local *Valley Morning Star* news-paper buries coverage of national and international news on page 7, crammed into 1, sometimes 2 pages on Sundays? Yet it takes a full 7 pages to encompass local high school sports? And the only time a team from Los Angeles gets a passing reference is when they are defeated by the Mavericks; stripped of their national collegiate football championship and Heisman Trophy by the NCAA; or a SoCal team is taken over by Major League Baseball's Commissioner as part of a settlement in a high-profile divorce?

When I Google driving directions from my address in Harl-ingen, the error message "location not found" keeps popping up. So I use the address of the steakhouse down the street as my starting location. The only time I had this problem in Los Ange-les was when I wasn't specific *enough*: since so many streets have the same names, and can wander endlessly for hundreds of miles through 50 different cities, you also need to include all ten digits of the zip code.

When you're looking for a job, it's a requirement here that you speak Spanish. Employers in the Rio Grande Valley should specify "Spanish" on their applications, though. I've been told the [true] story of a local woman who checked the "Bilingual" box on her employment application for a customer service posi-tion at a national retail chain. She was hired, but the first time she had to assist a customer who only spoke Spanish, she responded—in fluent German—and was fired later that same day.

This skill is still optional in LA,, although bilingual ability in Spanish is listed as "preferred" for many jobs, as well as Korean, Mandarin, Cantonese, Vietnamese, Russian and/or Farsi...

The pronouncements of my assimilation endeavors will continue.

SUSANNA GROVES

IMPORTANT CHICKENS (AND A BIRD)

I was about five visiting my family in Nuevo León, Mexico, and I cried when they took away the chicken that my great aunt had just given me. She was fat, and grey with red, and I held her in my arms. I loved that chicken, but they ended up eating her anyway, though I could not.

When we lived in Arizona, I killed a couple of my father's chickens. I was about six; I thought it was neat the way the chickens stopped moving when I twisted their neck. I threw the bodies over the fence where they plopped in the dust. My papa thought some animal had gotten them, and it caused a flurry of activity in our house, as he did not realize the animal had been me. The black hen and that plopping sound as her body landed was the last. I'd learned what I needed.

When we lived in Arizona my papa caught a roadrunner that beat itself bloody in its cage, wanting only to run along the road looking for lizards. And my papa took it out and put Vaseline on its wounds and set it free.

When we lived in West Texas, my papa fought his fighting cocks a few times. One of his favorites—black and wiry, very loved—failed in its fight, and my papa came home late. I ran into the night to meet him as he placed the battered corpse in the trash burning barrel and he lit one his Swisher Sweet cigars from the flame of the rooster burning away on top of the garbage and he never fought any of them again.

When we lived in the Valley, there were days when I would come home from school to find something had been killing my papa's gamecocks. The roosters would be dead with one foot tied to his string by his teepee. Finally, one day, what had been killing the chickens showed up—it was a golden eagle, the gigantic bird perched on a fence post wondering why he was not able to haul away his prey. I was in the backyard looking at it looking at me and I went back to the house and told my papa who grabbed his .22 rifle but couldn't shoot the eagle. We stood in the doorway looking at the magnificent bird, and my papa seemed to realize how it was: the eagle could no more resist his nature then the rooster could deny his. Thus the strings, so the backyard didn't turn into a battle royal of fighting cocks.

I remember my uncle, who was living in our garage, and my papa breaking the neck of a hen with flick of the wrist and then plucking her feathers, and then barbequing her. That time I did eat.

I remember when I found *Be Here Now* in my battleship's library and the story about a monk who is told by his master to take a chicken somewhere where no one can see and kill it. The monk left but came back to the master later and said 'I can't kill the chicken.'

The master asked 'Why?'

"Because, no matter where I go, the *chicken* is watching.'

'You have gained understanding'. . .

I stopped eating chicken in 1990 after seeing a film called *Faces of Death* showing the degrading dishonorable demise of industrialized raised chickens. They hung outside down throat slit, blood spraying and plucked while still sentient. Didn't do it again until 2000, maybe 'cause I lost my revulsion as I became more and more jaded with the world and it's not that I don't care, it's just with *so many* cares one gets hungry.

And *now* my son wants chickens . . .

JUVENTINO MANZANO

STRIDING THE BORDER

GLORIA ANZALDÚA AND *BORDERLANDS* MANIFESTO OF THE OUTSIDER

"Neither autonomy nor resistance are forms of organization and struggle which concern only the Indian peoples."

—Subcomandante Marcos
September 2002

In 1986 Gloria Anzaldúa's seminal work came onto the academic scene. This text was one that academics are to this day able to apply to many of the literary theories that would within the next decade dominate the course and discourse of English studies. The text in question *Borderlands—La Frontera—The New Mestiza,* is a book that even Anzaldúa herself refers to as "a feminist one" (106), yet I choose here to challenge the assumption she makes with the claim that this text is one of the outsider, the one who does not belong, the one standing in the corner, the one feeling out of place with the tone of the times, the dissident, the miscreant, the deviant, the culturally excluded, the sexually "abnormal." This is a book that blurs the distinctions between these groups.

In the introduction to the second edition, Sonia Saldívar-Hull says that *Borderlands* "continues to be studied and included on class syllabi in courses on feminist theory, contemporary American women writers, autobiography, Chicana/o and Latina/o literature, cultural studies, and even major American authors." This statement shows the immense impact this book has had on theory and the academic community at large. Saldívar-Hull does not mention that the book is a foundation of queer theory as well, and that the author herself through her works and actions has essentially "ostracized" herself as far as possible from the hegemonic cultural edifices attempting to dominate her culture. Anzaldúa, growing up, was presented with two cultures clashing discordantly over and over rather than melding harmonically, all around her in the Rio Grande Valley along the "border" of Texas and Mexico—*la frontera* (the frontier).

I want to look first at what Gloria Anzaldúa has done in order to create this text and then explain why I see it as a text for the proverbial outsider. Being in the physical location she is in she is able to see the cultural requirements placed upon her from two "rival" hegemonies: that of her Mexican background, and that of the American dominant culture, which seeks to demean the Mexican culture through various forms of degradation, or what Anzaldúa calls "Cultural Tyranny" (38). This Cultural Tyranny also relates to her own Mexican culture that expects and demands rigid paradigms and roles for the women and all Mexicans in general.

Meanwhile, "education," under the American hegemony for Mexicans, consists of being required to take classes in speaking English "like an American" or learning to ridicule the legends and stories of her own culture. "Back then, I, an unbeliever scoffed at . . . Mexican superstitions *as I was taught* in Anglo school" (italics mine 58). Anzaldúa as a Mexican woman was expected to adopt the roles of the Mexican culture and in these roles her freedom as a human being is incredibly limited. She first, then, has to make the break from the restraints of her own culture and then still have to face the restraints of the dominant paradigm that also demands fixed roles for women. Her first barrier is overcoming the sexism that exists in both cultures. Her rejection of the "rules" of her Mexican culture ostracizes her from its embrace. By "choosing" to be a lesbian she not only shatters the Mexican paradigm, but also shatters the "ruling" hegemony as well.

Now she is an outlaw and true outsider, not "fitting in" with either culture in the sexual role that has been preordained for her as a woman. Here we begin to see why this text is applicable, open, and an inspiration to such varied theory. We can begin to see that this is indeed a text from a frontier: a frontier of removal from the negative restraints of various hegemonies-- a new frontier in human awareness—a text of the outlaw, the outsider, and thus has far reaching appeal to not only women or queers but anyone who is part of the many disenfranchised people-- people who resist the "rules" and finding themselves outside of the mainstream. Cultures wanting to resist post-colonial imperialistic hegemony have much to learn from this book since the experiences are not unique to the Mexico/Texas border, but exist anywhere this clash of cultures occurs. Everywhere throughout the world in fact and in particular in the United States—the "melting pot" has left unassimilated. Everywhere these people exist: "The prohibited and forbidden are its inhabitants... the squint-eyes, the perverse, the queer, the troublesome, the mongrel, the mulatto, the half breed, the half dead, in short, *those who crossover pass over, or go through the confines of the "normal"* (italics mine 25).

I found that I could relate very strongly with this work, as I, too, am a *mestizo* having grown up in the same geographic conditions as Anzaldúa and sharing the blood of the dominant culture and the Mexican within my veins and have felt that same displacement; that existence in between—on the border. I am the product of the clash of the two cultures and my views on the world do not seem to fall into the mainstream of either culture, and I have felt the pressure throughout my life of the two cultures and never realized that it was such a thing that was suitable for study within the world of academia.

Having discovered this work labeled under ethnic studies, post-colonial studies and international studies, in a collection of literary theory, I realized that much of confusion I have felt about my place in the world could possibly be traced to this feeling of being caught in the middle—able to see the best and worst of two unique cultures and sympathizing with the routes taken by others to remove themselves from these monoliths: religion, state, school (Anzaldúa's "choosing" to become a lesbian, for example) and realizing that to simply call this a work of one of the above theories one i.e.: colonial studies or to simply call it feminist, is a bit shortsighted, as *Borderlands* is a text with almost unlimited power. My own rebelliousness towards organizations of all sorts must stem from my background as well. I have always wanted to subvert the ordinary and wanted to know the answer to the questions I asked for myself from experience rather than just because so and so said so. As Anzaldúa explains in one of the best ways I have ever found> "There is a rebel in me—the shadow-beast it is a part of me that refuses to take orders from outside authorities... It is the part of me that hates constraints of any kind, even those self-imposed. At the least hint of limitations on my time or space by others, it kicks out with both feet" (38). Yes, indeed. She speaks to me and to anyone who feels out of the loop with the dominant culture.

The paranoid paradigms of the state exist in order to form humans into the image they deem suitable for the "smooth" operation of the existing orders. Anyone offering forms of resistance, whether they be as Anzaldúa has done with her sexuality, or her throwing off of the disguises that were originally placed upon the old religious ways in order to aid in assimilation which when removed reveal the true nature of the culture, is turning themselves, in the eyes of the norm, into an outlaw. Outlaws, in a metaphoric sense have removed themselves from the realm of the everyday—they are doing what I believe Nie-

tzsche meant by a person being "beyond good and evil", breaking through the everyday and sending themselves into the fron-
tiers of raw human experience.

Anzaldúa has, by creating herself in her own image, "sided"
with the queers, feminists, Mexicans, the disenfranchised, dis-
possessed, the outlaw. This is a text done by an author who
speaks from a point of view of one striding over a vantage point
between the two clashing cultures, hiding in the netherworld of
the shadows, she is able to see the light that shines on the exposed, revealing a multitude of cracks and crevices that offer
refuge from the weight. She is able to look down at both cultures
catching them in the ways they attempt to enslave, and breaking
those chains for at least herself, and offering the insight and inspiration in her text to inspire us to do the same for ourselves.
She offers hope and resistance to all those who have suffered
under the boot of oppression. She gives us the message that we,
the outlaws will persevere. The oppressed and shamed will in-
herit what is left of the earth when the white hegemony collaps-
es, as she says:

> "*Los Chicanos*, how patient we seem, how very patient.
> There is the quiet of the Indian about us. We know how
> to survive. When other races have given up their
> tongue, we've kept ours. We know what it is to live un-
> der the hammer blow of the dominant *norteamericanao*
> culture. But more than we count the blows, we count
> the days the weeks the years the centuries the eons until
> the white laws and commerce and customs will rot in
> the desert they've created, lie bleached. *Humildes* yet
> proud, *quietos* yet wild, *nosotros los mexicanos*-
> Chicanos will walk by the crumbling ashes as we go
> about our business. Stubborn, persevering, impenetra-
> ble as stone, yet possessing a malleability that renders
> us unbreakable, we, the *mestizas* and *mestizos*, will re-
> main." (85-86)

Replace the Hispanic references and Anzaldúa speaks for all of us outsiders/outlaws, all of us not so likely to join the herd so busy working on their desert.

JUVENTINO MANZANO

VESTIGE TO VISAGE

"I'll send a message of death to the four winds. . ."
— "El Chivo" by El Coyote

The first time I saw Her I was 15 and it was at a deal my papa took me to in southern Nuevo Leon in order to introduce me officially to the mechanics of the family business. This wasn't just some "deal", this was a big deal—my papa was buying *tons* of marijuana and we were going to inspect and approve the transaction which his regional *patron* had set-up. My papa always carried a nickel plated Colt Combat Commander in .38 super, shiny as the moon seen through a hand lens. It had, until before this deal, silver *cachas* or grips, but now was decked out in ivory grips with Her carved in bas relief; wielding scythe and wearing Her cassock get up—a gift from a connection in Michoacán.

Everything was normal—just another day hanging with my papa even if it seemed unusual to be taken to a major deal, it was life. The sun was high, the mountain woods closed in around us and the air smelled of dried cannabis. Suddenly I could see we, the men with us, and the men from the other cartel all appearing as Her, but in different vestments— cowboy boots and hats, Levi's and shirts with fancy embroidery. My handsome papa, neatly trimmed black goatee, his brown eyes hiding layers he'd saved only for himself, his shirt with the marijuana leaves embroidered around the buttons open throated, anchor Christ necklace on his curly haired chest--Colt tucked into his belt--only the grips with Her visible.

As we toured the tonnage, I felt Her gaze on me from all the eyes around me—all the macho *narcos* fingering AK-47s and Colt's, their gold marijuana leaf necklaces, customized trucks parked idling, dual exhaust grumbling behind the shipment. It was a moment of revelation being able to see through Her eyes— understanding we were all as able as Her to wield the scythe without a second thought—reduced to reflex-ruthless. I remember it stronger than my first orgasm given to me by Angel in his pickup truck—him on the floor between my legs—tongue tapping a door I had not known existed crying out, "Epiphany," and I, "Angel"—a pleasant, perfect, continuous memory.

Money was exchanged; I was not introduced, just accepted without question. The farmer's representative, an old acquaintance of my papa, Don G, smiled when he saw me.

"*Mijita,* you are now a man." He grinned and I felt his eyes grope my breasts beneath my blouse.

My papa grinned ironically at his joke.

"So you know who you will eventually answer to."

"I never thought I would be someday answering to a woman, but as you say Don Puentes."

"It is not as I say; it is as it will be, never forget that." My papa patted his shoulder. "She will be majestically ruthless in my own fair way, as she is my reflection."

I felt myself blush under the gaze of my father, so full of love for me. I could feel his pride in waves coming off his hand resting lightly on my shoulder.

Don G looked at my papa then at me, raised his eyebrows, shook my hand, and kissed my cheek, too long.

He waved towards the neat bales of marijuana flowers.

"Beautiful, no?"

What could I say? Of course.

Being with my papa answered for all else, all internal questions. There was no mistaking who *he* was. Times were good back then--the law had been corrupted and *she* was on our side. Our cartel threw its share of once pointing-finger-floaters into the river and they would turn up like corks in a fruit bowl of sour champagne—eyes eaten out by fish, body bloated, filled with gas from the heat of the Northern Mexico Border sun which boiled them in the stagnant water rising their warning of death to the slow river's surface.

Every day he and I would pray to Her at our altar in the garden, light incense, leave cigarettes that would always be butts the next day, and pray to the *Virgen de Guadalupe* for my mother—lost during my entrance to the world.

My papa married his business after my mother's death, only attended to various mistresses, never bothering with another child as he said I was more than he could hope for from any child, and I could never view their subtle attempts at motherliness as anything more than attempts to transcend the fear they seemed to feel around me knowing they could never compete with the love a papa has for his only child.

The dreams began not too long after that first big deal. The first one came after doing a lot of coke with Angel and letting him take me to orgasm over and over again until I was a moaning-no-more-satiated-nymph-ravished-by-my-own-personal-Pan.

La Santa Muerte appeared to me in Her-grim-reaper-skeletal-glory asking for help. I was standing in a field of sunflowers—*girasoles*. She stood in dark contrast to the bright flowers motionless in Her presence.

"Help you?" I asked.

"Yes, help me. I miss my fleshly visage. I want it back again not this hideous skull, so frightening to so many, but my beautiful face that I so foolishly lost."

I felt no fear. I tried to look at Her face, in particular Her eyes, but all was in shadow even in this field lit so brightly by the namesake flower's friend.

"I will show you my true beauty when you work for me to regain the flesh I have lost. I need more blood to run; I need to regain the respect of those who think that incense will satisfy my appetite."

"I don't know what I can do."

"Oh yes you do."

The sunflowers started spinning on their stems—a mass of brilliant windmills spinning with no wind to spin them. That was the first time. I woke heart beating fast, still seeing the spinning flowers before my half opened eyes. I waited for my heart to calm and returned to a static, dreamless sleep.

I asked my papa about the *Santa Muerte*. He explained that like so much of the religion of Mexico, She was a cover for the worship of ancient gods—in Her case, it seemed to my father She was the present "incarnation" of the Aztec god *Mictlan-tecuhtli* who was the "Mr. Death" of the *Mexica,* shared a similar countenance, and seems to have been much attentive to his followers than the weak gods of the Spanish, at least until the conquest when all the old gods seemed to have fled in fear of the paper sky god of the Spanish. I remarked that she/he must have been well fed during the Conquest—perhaps she enjoyed the decimation of her worshippers by the bloody steel horsed Spaniards who inadvertently fed her/him well through inquisition in the name of their bloody God and his tortured Son—better than Her worshippers ever had. It seemed to me that She had let them perish—perhaps they had tried to appease Her with incense. She was a vestige of something older than what we knew—a terrible truth that the Spanish had destroyed when confronted, had risen once more, no longer afraid of the gaze of the Christians and ready and willing to receive blood again instead of Christ's weak metaphorical wine for Her sustenance, and that of Her worshippers. My Papa hugged me and said that

I was always asking questions instead of just accepting. It was not a woman's place to question a man, but being his daughter, he said, allowed me the right to be more than any man.

The dreams haunted me as I grew older. Eventually I went to the States to study at university and She was quiet while I investigated philosophy which confirmed there were no answers to any of my existential questions and also learned that the belief system of mine and my father's was not something to be discussed with the typical watery brained American. I made the mistake of talking honestly about what I knew of *Santa Muerte*, Kali, Vishnu, the Virgin, and the other supposed mythos my father had instilled in me with my dorm mate and the conversation ended with my brutal punctuation mark of a slap on the young woman's face after she said my father had poisoned and perverted me and that without the words of Christ, I was lost. I told her to have her soggy, weak savior come and wipe the blood from her face. I had wanted to crush this *gringa*, but her bloody nose sufficed. She ended up moving to a different room.

I realized upon my return to my father's *hacienda* with my ineffectual B.A. in philosophy and logic, She had been with me back when Angel, my too-cute, cokehead boyfriend, would drive around wired out of his mind listening to *corridos* super loud in his yellow customized "coke" truck with an AK-47 in the gun rack. And I, a bit timid around him, would sit next to him—too sweaty, his satin shirt sticking to him, his arm around me telling me to hit the vial of coke left wet with his mucus, until he took us somewhere to garner more experience together in the pleasures of the flesh—and I wondered if She missed those things.

She was with us when I accompanied Angel and two of his goons, Ram and Gary, wasted on marijuana, tequila, and cocaine, on a scare-the-shit-out-of-'em, drive-by AK-47 ranting rapid Kalashnikov broken words of warning leaving broken windows and blood splatters behind like an audience that had fainted headfirst in the afterglow of its immense, cigarette-lighting, muzzle flash. Angel drove off laughing into the night, the hot brass from the rifle a trail of crumbs behind us. I laughed numbly, feeling Her without knowing what I was feeling.

I realized She had been with me when Tiva and I had taken massive quantities of mushrooms during a stupid Spring Break celebration at South Padre Island before we became wise to the stupidity of all those inane frat boys and beer bonging sorority girls getting blasted on the beach and how we almost wandered into a gang-bang, but we felt Her, and even though the boy that Tiva was talking to was really cute, there was no way we would go into the condo where the light from a porno movie on a big screen TV blasted its pale fleshy light out into the night. We spent the rest of the night at one of those open 24 hour American restaurants eager to fill our bellies with fattening, greasy food. We drank coffee and smoked instead, ducking into the restroom to blaze a one-hitter, hoping the boy did not follow us.

So uneven in her appearances, yet there was always the thread of death in all those scenarios—of either me or someone else in my path. I often wonder how many people lived in fear of my father and his cartel and how did they respond when they felt Her presence. Did they sit and think of those bullets hitting the walls and windows or their house and realize that they were Santa Muerte's nails running down her lover's back?

DURING THE TIME I was in America, *Santa Muerte* became almost mainstream back home, as mainstream as a skeletal goddess worshipped by criminals and *narcos* could become. There were comics about her, books legitimizing Her worship, shrines arose feeding Her ego, and offerings given up daily from various cartels throughout the country leaving their mark on the world of violence—echoing, yet transcending the crimes of those we admired—those prohibition gangsters and the corrupt government agencies from the roaring twenties and the time of concrete shoes and St. Valentine massacres, and as Her offerings increased, She gained power, fed well by all of us, She entered more lives as though She had always been the dominant force behind them. And the irony was that She was.

The *narco* business had changed too. It had been the hippies and their weed, trying to change the world in their idealistic way thinking turning everyone on would suffice, a noble attempt—they were mind manifesting--but now it seemed the North Americans had developed a heavier appetite for less mind manifestation and more mind removal—as though the way of life they led, so devoid of family, culture, even good food, took a tremendous toll on their happiness. Yet they persisted in pursuing the worship of *things* while they drowned themselves in heroin, cocaine, speed and lots and lots of pharmie drugs—the new favorites, in order to live a numbed and nullified existence—on those pills one could put up with anything and it seemed to make television, which I personally shunned, even more bearable as an escape for the unhappy *gringos*.

She appeared in my room one night shortly after I had returned to my papa's house wearing Her robe without Her scythe. No words were spoken—She was now a visage of flesh, not bone, and was quite beautiful. Over Her cassock She wore a medallion of Kali, a Christ on an anchor, a marijuana leaf in silver, and a coke spoon. She rattled as She walked to my bed. Empathy in waves came off of Her—I could feel nothing but silence-stillness. She wanted to keep this fleshy face. I needed to feed Her; I needed to do what would give Her what She wanted—a face of Her own, always. Her eyes where felt but not seen as they were hidden in the dark from falling shadows of Her hood and hair, yet they still managed to rake mine leaving me to contemplate the feeling She imparted.

It was like being a woman was what She knew—She smelled me, breathing in my scent. I did not succumb to Her without a grimace and She nodded touching my head—I knew Her from somewhere besides Her iconic image at the altar and I recognized the feeling as the one I felt when I cried out to Angel and when I detected the look of Her in those long ago men at that inaugural deal.

"Do you see what I could bring you every night?"

I did not say anything, but let Her continue touching me.

"This without the demands of the men, those demands that are for their own selfish means—they use, I only give and only demand my favor is returned in blood. That is all."

I let Her take me again and again. And She did. And I never saw Her eyes, all I wanted to see.

Later I awoke with the moon streaming in my window—my curtain blew inward and then like a lung breathing filled with air, went outward into the night. The moon, bright as muzzle flash, seemed to sigh. I went back to sleep after masturbating, dreaming of my papa's .38 super.

How Freudian it seemed to me, but then I realized that it was like a king's scepter; the ruled dream of the scepter, the ruler dreams to be rid of it. I would gladly take it if it would result in the visage retaining flesh and not simply bone. It seemed flesh I would like to see every day and Her eyes, just the thought of them on me, gazing into mine, were enough to drive a person crazy. One could not see them, yet, even unseen I *felt* I had seen them and they were silent, vast as the universe, as known as the back of your hand, but one could not be sure.

"He's going after Michoacán first. What a surprise. I wonder how Don G will handle things. How many of his own networks is this bastard betraying?"

My father was letting questions fly as we watched the TV showing federal troops in military issue Hummers peering over machine guns inadvertently blaring the message of *La Santa Muerte* all over the screen as their fellow troops kicked in a door or searched a car, or set up a roadblock where perhaps, they themselves, the troops wired on speed, stoned, and drunk could have a private party under the authority of the state.

We watched as the news woman, a tall blond Aryan type with large breasts smiled as she relayed how a major cartel boss had been captured at his mistress's house in his underwear. It was quite the hoot.

"They have no honor, these federal *mamones* striking as we sleep."

"No papa, they have no honor."

My papa looked at me and reached over and kissed my cheek.

"My daughter" He stroked my hair. "You make me so proud."

"Papa, I only speak what I know is truth."

My papa smiled and sat back in his chair.

"This bastard is using his troops, lackeys really, as a private police force to shake down the cartels that must not have paid tribute or knew too much about him to allow them to stand. Don't you think it is funny it is his home state he hits first? Perhaps favors needed repaying, but this was more convenient."

The blond woman had been replaced by a commercial for some breakfast cereal covered in sugar from the States. A large menacing tiger sprinkled what looked like cocaine on the flakes of corn and a young white looking girl smiled eagerly as she pushed a spoonful of entirely synthetic crap into her mouth.

We both knew, as did everyone else in the cartels, that it was not about getting tough on *narcos*—it was just about power for this new president and assuredly some sort of monetary grant from the *Norteamericanos* for fighting the "war on drugs." Which every narco knows is what keeps us in business. Cartels fear legalization, like vampires garlic.

My father said this man would be the undoing of the relative peace that existed as long as things were kept in balance—not one family, nor group could have all the power—it had to be spread about—intermingled with money and position and family. But when you try to put ideology on what has always been the way, you end up on the lap of the pretentious- self-righteous-talking-of-crusades-and-wars-against-things-he-could-not-comprehend-president of the States, to be turned into a tiny lap dog poodle stroked by bloody, money covered hands, and we had to engage in war with the cartels the president had deemed loyal to his agendas. While we were cursed having seen through the transparent words that he spoke, words simply vindicating him as our new capitalist savior and stoolie for our neighbor to the north that provided so much of our business.

My dreams of Santa Muerte during this time had been increasing in intensity and made me more insistent than I could have been without. I would wake shuddering feeling as though I'd come—nervous, anxious, and then returned to sleep seeing shells ejecting from my father's .38 super, its muzzle flashing brighter than a camera flash leaving imprints on my eyes.

My father gave in to Angel and his father's insistent appeals that together we would be stronger, there would be more profit for both, and we could expand on all fronts, controlling all aspects of the *narco* trade, at least along the northern states, in particular our home state of Nuevo Leon. We would also be able to cause more death to those who would oppose the normal nature of things. We became even better armed and more ruthless towards the police who got in our way—we even broadcast our murders on the internet—warnings seen worldwide.

One night not too long after we started to move cocaine and heroin She came to me and showed me She was pleased with the direction we were going, but still insisted I could do more for Her to insure Her the face She knew I desired. Our affair was to continue and She promised I would even get to see Her eyes. She showed me in a nightmare inside a dream what She wanted of me:

I shot my father and dumped him as a floater. He was found two days later with the front of his face missing, quite bloated. It was not as difficult as it sounds since my papa had complete trust in me and no doubt in whatever was left of his consciousness at the impact of the bullet; he imagined it was a sniper and hoped I made it out. The only witness was me and the Colt, her image on the grips in my calm, detached, caressing-her-hand. Even blindfolded I would have seen, and even with my hands over her eyes I know she saw the muzzle flash—

it burned my eyes like a lightning flash freezing, leaving it ringing, like my ears, that oddly myopic moment in my mind.

I kept the empty shell that ejected. I picked it up from the river bank, my chintzy dime store prize brilliant as the tears that I left in the dirt bursting in prisms through my waterfall eyes. Blood speckled my blouse sleeve--delicate red filigree lace encircling my murdering hand. I knew this would not be all, in the end, and his body's splashing entrance into the river announced my own descent.

I awoke shaking. I could never do that. Could I? I could be the queen of it all. I could kill my father and start a war as our world had never seen. I did not think I could do so, but *La Santa Muerte* said I must.

I wanted to insure the gaze of those eyes would be mine, though--like a basilisk I intended to have that as mine so that I could now tell this story to you. I could dwell with the fleshy visage in Her reign even greater than my papa. As the war picked up, Angel's father was killed and on that night She came again-- resplendent in Her wedding gown. She had changed from hassock to this and She was beautiful, but no eyes could be seen on Her, even with no hood a shadow covered Her face and there was no doubt that the new president worked for Her and made Her smile grandly, floaters made Her smile, that the dead police made Her grin, and even our own who wrought the same as we wrought and ended up heading to that great silence made Her laugh, but I knew that what was wanted of me after Her taking me to the brink over and over until She left me writhing weak and worn out. I was to wield the .38 super with the authority of Zeus if I was to take it from my father. I woke the next morning with a whole set of luggage under my eyes which I covered with makeup, something I abhorred wearing, but I knew then, that I must take my father's pistol from him. His stainless steel Colt Combat Commander .38 Super—his life.

I was not prepared to do that. Give Her myself, even though I had—Her touch kept me going. Angel wondered why I no longer sought him out, but did not seem too disturbed, in fact he was not as insistent in making love to me as he had been and only murmured that it did not really matter if he showed his love in this realm or not.

To me, his love was pale in comparison to Hers. But I knew She lied to me, that She would never show me those eyes She kept hidden, instead reverting to Her fearful image and telling me that I was not the only one. I knew it then, She lied to me, and every time I dream of Her since the death of my papa dream, She smiles and bites me on the hand that holds the Colt telling me to do it and then take what is ours to take and with misplaced wrath our cartel will wipe out all rivals leaving blood and tears on the mourner's faces and sweat on the back of pall bearers who were being called in at a professional capacity to fill in the gaps of our rival's loses and Her face would be more youthful, eyes still hidden in shadow.

Her, all about Her ego--it seemed that She transposed Her own desires onto me—that She would have the fleshly face She so demanded, now—and it now seems She asked all of worshippers the same thing—extended the same cards to all keeping it secret between them that they were not getting the unique deal they thought they were and that no matter what, She would be the winner in Her cosmic card game. This realization came too late to inspire anything more than the hope I would leave this dream quickly—and so in the end, I ironically begged Her, to even so, please, make me come quickly.

MY FATHER AND I went to see Don G and on our way back from touring the plants he grew so well, I told my father I brought extra shells and wanted to pistol shoot—see if I am still as good a shot as I once was. He had once told me before I had gone to University that I was not only a wonderful poet, but a fine shot. A child any papa would be proud of, and here we are shooting *Tecate* beer cans that had been floating around in the back of my papa's pickup here on this beautiful beach outside of Matamoras, the gulf infinite—no telling where the sky began and the ocean ended.

"Here, Epiphany, shoot mine, I will shoot yours."

I had a .45 Colt that I had bought with financial aid money and smuggled back to Mexico.

"Oh, papa, I would love to."

"Epiphany, you know mine is yours."

I nodded and took his pistol. He went and set up cans towards the retreating morning ocean, his back to me I aimed his shiny pistol at him. I had his inverted triangle back in the combat sites. I lowered the gun and pointed it at an innocuous seashell residing on the sand.

"Are you ready?"

My voice nearly broke, "Yes, papa."

The cans were set up and my father stood behind me as I fired instinctively knocking over all eight without a glitch, loving the milder recoil of the .38 super.

"Beautiful, you still are my poetic gunslinger. Go again."

He went back to set up the mutilated cans again. The sun was getting heavier above us. Seagulls rushed away. Over his back, She appeared big as the Virgin of Guadalupe resplendent in Her wedding dress, eyes obscured by the sun, above my papa, outlined in an aura of purple and black. She beckoned with Her finger, inciting me to shoot my papa as he set up the cans whistling a *narcocorrido*.

I reloaded the .38 super's magazine expertly dropping the empty to the sand. I fired all 8 rounds into the image of La Santa Muerte above him, who recoiled, growled, and disappeared, in less than the three seconds it took to fire off the magazine. My papa had dropped to the sand pulling out my own .45 in less than the time it had taken me to empty his gun.

"*Mijita!* What the hell are you doing?" My papa cried out waving my .45 towards me.

"There was a big ugly seagull about to poop on you." I giggled.

My father looked around him.

"I see nothing."

"What else would you expect from your poetic-gunslinger-only- daughter, my dear papa?"

"Next time warn me, my dear. You scared the proverbial devil out of me."

"Sorry, Papa." I had a rock of love in my throat. "Papa?"

He stood up and dusted sand off his pants and put the .45 back in his waistband. "Yes, *hija*?"

"I want to go to grad school back in the States."

That was the last time I saw *La Santa Muerte*. I have been back to visit my papa who still runs the show and we have had great times. I no longer dream of Her. My cartel found out later that Angel had his father killed in order to escalate the violence and he could not say why he choose to do such a thing even as he was tortured to death by members of his own cartel. But I think I know why.

JUVENTINO MANZANO

BRINGING DOWN THE WITCH

Jesús María Benítez twisted on his mount to glance back at Captain Thomas Douglas, a towering man when on foot and even more imposing astride his enormous, black Arabian stallion, its finely wrought saddle gleaming with silver and festooned with the flopping, macabre scalps of a dozen Comanche. Like many Ranger captains, Douglas was a man whose time had apparently passed: with the signing of the Treaty of Guadalupe Hidalgo two years ago, after Texas's annexation and the end of the war, the newly inducted state had little need for its warriors. The federal Indian Agents had stepped in, and the governor seldom called Ranger companies up for service.

In answer to this callous abandonment, the captain had found a just cause here in the northern extremes of Mexico: protecting its citizens from Comanche raiders that had begun boldly to surge into Mexican territory. Now he carried himself even more erectly and proudly than he had as an officer. Behind him, his men—some sixteen former Texas Rangers and American soldiers, plus one or two men of checkered pasts and mixed race—were arrayed in a casual triangle with Douglas at the apex. Their saddle bags too were decorated with bloody bunches of black hair: the troop had had the good fortune to come upon a Comanche camp several miles south of the border, well below the areas the Comanche themselves had agreed to as their territory, and Douglas had ordered the men, mostly older warriors, and any women without infant children slaughtered and scalped. The rest they had driven across the river and back into the U.S.

The troops' spirits were high, as each scalp would fetch some fifty dollars from the Mexican government, but Jesús María's stomach churned with fear. The scalping had been so easy because the band's warriors were out on a raid, perhaps even as far south as Saltillo, where it was said one could see the Indians walking boldly on the streets, laughing at the cowardice of the inhabitants of that city. They were gone, but they would soon be back, and Jesús María wanted himself and his old mare as far from the scene of the slaughter as possible. His mother, who had died when he was young precisely at the hands of Comanche warriors, had taught him a little of the old magic, and he discreetly made signs of power in the air, spells of protection meant to ward off the prying eyes of mediums. Any animal, he knew, could be the spy of a Comanche witch: the large hordes of Comanche that had been filtering into northern Mexico for the last six months or so were rumored to be led by just such an ancient sorceress. And even were there no wizened, magical crone at its head, that race was notorious for its ability to understand the whisperings of creatures and plants and rocks: Jesús María would take no chances.

Close to nightfall they reached a stand of mesquite trees atop a gently sloping knoll and dismounted to set up camp. Still watchful, Jesús María, guide and cook for this particular group of gringos, started a low, unobtrusive fire and prepared beans with chili and fatback. After he had served the men, he walked quietly along the perimeter of the camp, casting about for any sign that they'd been followed. He was so intent on his search that he did not hear Douglas approach. *Stupid*, he thought to himself in Spanish. *Had he been an Indian, I'd be dead.*

"Jesús."

"Yes, Captain?"

"What are you doing?" The Captain was sipping from a flask of bourbon.

"Checking for that we not followed, sir."

"Well, of course we weren't followed!" A mix of indignation and good humor winked in the gringo's eyes. "You think this is the first time me and my men have been in a dangerous situation? Come on back to the fire; tell us a story. Brady's got the watch, and he'll tell us if he sees something."

Jesús María sighed softly and looked up at the clear sky as if to beg God sarcastically to forgive him for ever getting involved with these careless, liquor-drinking Texans. That's when he saw it: a little light, dimmer than a star but closer to them, moving slowly across the sky in erratic spirals.

"Oh, hellfire, Captain, look at!" he pointed at the black expanse of night. "The light yonder that it keeps on a-moving round and round! You see it, Captain?"

Douglas tilted his head back. "Yes, I do. A shooting star, I reckon."

"No, no shooting star, sir: that's a witch."

Douglas smirked condescendingly. "You people sure are superstitious, aren't you? There's no witches flying about these parts, nor anywhere else, for that matter."

Jesús felt his heart thumping wildly like some primitive drum. He clapped his hand to his chest, worried that his own fear might call the witch's attention. Perhaps she had already spied them. What if she was working with the Comanche? Together with the inexplicable upswing in Comanche activity here in northern Mexico and the stories of the witch that had initiated their intrusions, rumors had been going around for months now about one particular band led by a warrior dressed in *charro* garb, the silver-crusted sable of the finest Spanish horsemen. Jesús had learned since a child to fear charros as potential infernal agents. His mother, fleeing steadily northward with her young son, leaving the state of Morelos and an abusive father far behind, had instructed him to be wary of the black-geared, fancy rider: like the skeletal *calaca* or the Spanish dandy, this charro was an avatar of Satan. Such a being was certainly aided by *naguales*, shape-shifting witches, most commonly in the form of large screech owls.

Jesús María's thoughts whirled chaotically as he tried to grapple with the crisis at hand. With a hope-filled gasp, he remembered what *mamá* had taught him nearly two decades previously in their humble *choza* on the outskirts of Monterrey, just months before being murdered by a Comanche brave. He had been only ten years old, but she had already begun to show him the powerful defenses, the intricate spells that would keep him safe. He could see her now clearly in his mind's eye, her delicate fingers undoing her blouse, dark eyelashes shut against the physical world. He had shivered at her murmured words, but he had learned his lesson well. A way to guard oneself from evils above. *A way to capture a witch.*

"We got to bring her down, Captain Douglas, sir."

Douglas snorted in laughter. "Dang, Jesús, you gone and made bourbon come out my nose! Bring her down? Why, even supposing she is a witch, why bring her down? And how?"

"Why?" Jesús thought of mentioning the charro, but decided against it. "Cause she maybe is working with the braves that we kilt their people. How? Well, like this."

Benítez began to pull off his clothes: poncho, cotton shirt, twill pants. The other Texans saw him stripping and came closer, hooting and making fun.

"That's right, Jesús, give us a show!" one of them yelled, and the others guffawed. Jesús María ignored them and started putting on his clothes, but backwards.

"Boy, you been drinking, or what?" someone asked amid uproarious laughter. "Don't forget to spin that sombrero arsy-versy, too, Chuy!"

Their guide, nodding seriously, spun his wide-brimmed hat around and began to mumble. "*Amen. Oeternam. Vitam. Resurrectionem. Carnis.*" All laughter was smothered by his hoarse whispering. Heavy with power, the ancient words wormed their way thickly into the chill night air, and more than one Texan shivered to hear them.

"What's he saying, Cap?" a young ex-cowhand named Baker asked under his breath.

Jesús María ignored them and continued his raspy chant: "*Communionem sanctorum. Catholicam ecclesiam sanctam.*" The air grew electric with each murmured word.

"Hang on, boys. Wait: I think..."

"*Sanctum Spiritum in Credo.*"

"You know, I do believe he's saying the *credo*, the Apostle's Creed that Catholics recite. Had to learn it myself, back before Texas independence, so I could become a Mexican citizen. Yep, it's the *credo*, only he's saying in backward, and in Latin."

The men stared dumbly as Jesús María labored to pronounce the words. As he reached the end of the incantation, their guide again inclined his face upward and saw the light begin to fall. "Look at!" he shouted, pointing. Collectively, their eyes followed the bright blur as it streaked toward the ground some forty yards away. A soft thud trembled in the soles of their boots.

"Well, I'll be," muttered Douglas. "I think Jesús here just brought him down a witch!" He began running toward the site of the impact, the smaller Mexican right behind him. Lying in the yellow scrub grass they found the backbone of a cow.

"What in eternal damnation?" Douglas exclaimed softly.

Jesús María knelt beside the bone. "Help me, Captain. We got to carry this back to the trees for we could tied it up there. You'll see, trust me."

A couple of the other men lent a hand and soon they were wrapping a length of rope around the spine and one of the mesquite trees. Everyone worked in silence, and Jesús María could tell they were afraid. "Don't worry none. We got her now. She ain't gonna say nothing right now, but by morning, she'll show herself to us, I promise y'all."

Nervous and muttering to each other, the men settled down to sleep. Douglas tried to stay awake, but Jesús watched him nod off in starts until the captain was snoring like the rest. Brady's watch finished, and the Texan woke Robert Jones. Jesús sipped his coffee and observed the young man, making his circuit around the camp, but always glancing backward at the spiny whiteness affixed to the tree. Jesús María himself felt a similar anxiety, and that was why he refused to let sleep take him. *That witch would try to sneak into my dreams and seduce me*, he thought. *Best I stay awake till morning.* It was difficult: the gleaming white of the bone brought images of blood-streaked craniums exposed to sunlight under the gringos' knives. He tried reminding himself of his mother's mutilated corpse, the primary reason for his becoming a guide for scalp-hunters, the obsession that had compelled him to accept Douglas's offer late that summer. Nonetheless, exhaustion and caffeine combined to make his memories vividly phantasmagoric: Comanche corpses seemed to leer at him from the darkness, but he dared not close his eyes.

Eyes closed. *Lady Justice.* The captain was always holding forth on this ideal: the blind goddess, he called her, and he extolled her in a way he never did any other woman. Jesús María was not so naïve, despite being twenty-five years younger than the hardened warrior: what they did was not justice- it was vengeance. And vengeance always begat vengeance in a never-ending cycle: this was but another link in the chain. Unwittingly, the Texans had helped the young Mexican avenge his mother's death time and again, and the phantoms that plagued his aching mind seemed to promise that life would soon come full circle.

The watch changed twice more before the sun sent streaming heralds of gold and red into the sky. Jesús María turned to watch the sunrise, and when he turned back, she was there. Startled, he rushed to awaken the captain.

"Well, just look at that," Douglas murmured appreciatively as he pulled on his boots and lit a cigar. Instead of a cow's backbone, a beautiful young Mexican girl, light-complected and about seventeen or so, struggled with the ropes that held her to the mesquite. Jesús reached out a hand to stop the captain from walking too close to her, but the giant man simply shrugged him off. "What's your name, missy?" When she didn't reply, he asked again in Spanish: "¿Cómo se llama?"

She stared at him with wide, imploring eyes, and answered in that language. "*Azucena Hernández*," she whispered. "*Oh, please, sir, let me go. My father will kill me if he finds out!*"

"*What, that you are a witch?*"

She began to sob, just as Jesús had expected. Quickly, urgently, he muttered in English, "Don't listen to her, *jefe*. She wants to confuse you for that you could let her go. She's lying, whatever she says."

"*I am not a witch!*" Azucena cried. "*I, I just learned to fly so I could visit my boyfriend. We live so far apart, and I hardly ever get to see him. Oh, please believe me, sir. I promise I will never do it again! I know it is wrong, that it is of the Devil. I just love him so much. I promise: let me go, and I will walk away from here and never ever fly again!*"

Sighing, Jesús shook his head. "You got to burn her, Captain. Even for you Protestants, the Bible tells you not to be letting a witch live." He gestured at a couple of the men. "Come on, y'all: help me to gather the firewood."

Douglas was staring into the girl's green doe eyes, trembling as they were with tears not yet shed. He took a step toward her, then another; reaching out, he let his fingers graze her cheek. With a shudder, he called to his men. "No. No collecting firewood. We're letting her go."

As the captain drew his Bowie knife, Jesús objected. "Douglas, you never had no problem killing bad peoples before, sir. Why you want to save this girl? You saw her fly, you know that she done used magic to transform herself, too. You can kill Comanche, but not a pretty *güera* witch?"

But it was too late. Douglas seemed not to hear a word his guide said. With a single deft movement, he sliced the knots, and the rope fell away from Azucena as if recoiling in fear. She rubbed her arms, looking down humbly at the ground. Then she raised her head slowly and looked Jesús María right in the eyes, seeing into his soul, a smile pulling mischievously at her cheeks.

"*Nos vemos pronto*," she mouthed, leaping into the air and twisting into a glowing ball that sped away, sucking air after it in gasping streams and ripping the troops' hats from their heads. *See you soon.* Jesús choked off a sob.

The knife slipped from Captain Douglas' hand as he stared at the receding light. His features darkled with gradual comprehension. He sank to his knees slowly. "What have I done, Jesús?"

Jesús María's heart no longer even bothered to bang against his ribs. It knew it had little time left to beat. "She is with the braves, Tomás. She goes now for to tell them of us. We kilt their women and old men, and now they're gonna pay us back." The others blanched in fear. Jesús almost mentioned the satanic charro then, but he knew it little mattered whether they understood what was coming for them.

"We should to try and run," he finally muttered, though he knew flight was useless. Some of the men hurriedly mounted, leaving bedroll and supplies behind, and raced off. Douglas remained kneeling between the trees. Jesús María walked over and sat beside him. Already he could hear the approaching hoof beats.

"She was so beautiful, Jesús. And I could feel her in my heart." The captain closed his eyes then opened them wide in understanding. "Oh, my friend. You were right. Justice isn't blind, is she. She sees all too well."

The guide said nothing, just crossed himself silently and waited. Soon the first mustang came charging over the hill, and from Jesús María's chapped lips a little childlike moan escaped. It was a Comanche warrior with a naked, paint-streaked torso, but the chaps and silver-bangled *sombrero* of a charro. In his right hand he hefted a crooked spear, its tip jagged black obsidian fringed by a ruff of sable feathers; his red, unsaddled mustang bore down on Jesús like hell itself. Above the brave's head, harrowing the men with a sepulchral cry, an ashen screech owl beat enormous wings against the darkness. Its eyes were luminescent green.

Jesús María closed his own eyes in resigned submission.

"See you soon, mamá," he whispered. The he began the *credo* again, the way it was meant to be said: "*Credo in Deum Patrem omnipotentem.*"

He never reached the end. The warrior swung the shield on his left arm around, and Jesús María saw his reflection in an obsidian mirror mounted in its center, a reflection of his own soul, twisted by hate and fear, his wispy soul that now clung uselessly to the world as the shiny, inexorable black stone wrenched it from the flesh and dragged it into the darkness beyond.

DAVID BOWLES

DRAMA
SELECTION

NIGHT BY THE RIVER

CAST

María
Sofía
Luis
Pablo

Scene I - *Sofía's house. Lights up on bare stage with María holding a mirror. Sofía is helping her prim her hair.*

SOFÍA
María, *m'ija*, you are so beautiful. But you are getting too old.

MARÍA
Mama, nineteen is not old!

SOFÍA
All of your friends have already been married and have had at least two kids. What is taking you so long? Huh? Most young women get married by fifteen. You know this!

MARÍA

Mama, stop. The men in this town are pigs. They are dirty, smelly men with absolutely no class. *Nada.*

SOFÍA

María, this is what our village has to offer. Why can't you be happy with the men here?

MARÍA

Have you not seen them? They are so fat. Ugh. And lazy. That Pablo Martínez, he will not leave me alone. I have already told him so many times. No means no.

SOFÍA

Why don't you give him a chance? He's such a sweet young man. He's hard working. And his father owns the most land in the village.

MARÍA

Mama, I don't care. I don't like him.

SOFÍA

So? Are you just going to wait for a man to fall into your lap?

MARÍA

No. (*beat*) Have you ever seen a Frenchman? I heard that they will sweep you off your feet, go to work all day for you and treat you like a queen.

SOFÍA

Where did you hear all of this nonsense?

MARÍA

Ay, mamá, in the story books!

SOFÍA

María, you know those are rubbish and they only put funny ideas in your head. Don't read that stuff. You should spend your time getting a man.

MARÍA

But mamá, wouldn't it be nice to sit around all day, get fat and have Frenchman take care of you?

SOFÍA

Oh, you can get fat without a Frenchman. Now c'mon, you are going to be late. (*Suddenly working faster*)

MARÍA

Ow! Mamá, stop that! I'm pretty enough already, I don't need more brushing.

SOFÍA

María, you better stop talking that way!

MARÍA

Ay, what way, mamá?

SOFÍA

Saying you're pretty all the time.

MARÍA

You don't think I am pretty?

SOFÍA

Of course, *m'ija*, but other people don't like to hear it. Understand?

MARÍA

They are just jealous.

SOFÍA

¡Ay! Maybe they are and maybe they aren't! Just try to watch what you say.

MARÍA

Yes, mamá.

SOFÍA

Now, c'mon or we're going to be late.

MARÍA

What's the rush? It's only a village dance. The same people every time. The same fat, smelly men, trying to get me with beer breath.

SOFÍA

Stop being this way; you never know who you might see.

MARÍA

Pablo I'm sure. All night! Mamá, he won't leave me alone. And don't you be mad at me if I run as soon as I see him.

SOFÍA

Would you stop being so sassy?

MARÍA

Fine.

SOFÍA

No, go. *¡Ándale!*

(The two leave stage left.)

Scene II - *Next scene begins at a festive dance with music off in the distance.* ***María*** *has isolated herself away from the dance and sits herself on a bench.* ***Luis*** *enters.*

LUIS

Oh, excuse me. I wasn't aware that anyone was here.

MARÍA

Oh.

LUIS

I'm sorry, my name is Luis. Luis de la Garza. And you?

MARÍA

María. (*He kisses her hand. She tries to be "stand-off-ish" but there is a mild interest.*)

LUIS

Just María, huh? (*She doesn't answer*) So, you don't like danc-ing?

MARÍA

No, I just don't like the company.

LUIS

Me!? I'm sorry, I --

MARÍA

No, someone else.

LUIS

Oh. Oh, good. May I ask who?

MARÍA

Just this really annoying man. You don't know him.

> LUIS

Try me.

> MARÍA

Pablo.

> LUIS

Pablo?

> MARÍA

Yes, Pablo, the guy with green shirt and dirty sombrero.

> LUIS

Pablo Martínez?

> MARÍA

Yes.

> LUIS

That's my cousin.

> MARÍA

Huh, I guess you do know him.

> LUIS

Oh yeah, we used to play together when he lived near Veracruz.

> MARÍA

I'm sorry. I didn't mean to offend you.

> LUIS

Don't worry about it. He's always drunk. He does it to himself.

MARÍA

(*Beat*) You know I haven't seen you here before, and believe me, I always notice new faces.

LUIS

How's that?

MARÍA

Because there aren't any.

LUIS

(*Laughs*) I'm from Veracruz, but Pablo told me that the farming would be better here. Especially across the river. (*Points over his shoulder*)

MARÍA

Yes, I heard that. So...you live here now then?

LUIS

Sí, with Pablo. He didn't give me much of a room, but it's what I have until I can better fend for myself.

MARÍA

I take it you were a farmer back in Veracruz?

LUIS

Yes. I was pretty good at it until the drought. But farming did teach me one valuable lesson—don't let anything get in the way of your success.

MARÍA

That's good.

LUIS

Sí.

(*Long uncomfortable pause. **Pablo** barges in drunk.*)

PABLO
Oh, hey Luis. María (*Seductively*). Are we here to dance or what?

LUIS
Would you like to go back to the dance now or did you want to stay—

MARÍA
I'll go with *you.*

LUIS
¿De veras?

MARÍA
Sí.

(*He takes her hand and leads her back towards the dance.
Pablo sneers at them and exits in drunken stupor.
End scene.*)

Scene III - Opens in **Luis** and **María's** home. He is trying to rest and the baby is making noise.)

LUIS
María! María! Dammit, I'm trying to rest! Please keep that thing quiet!

MARÍA
(*Entering with baby in cloth*) Thing? Luis, this is our son!

                              LUIS

Look, I know, María, I know. But for the past three days, all it
has done is scream!

                              MARÍA

What do you expect from a newborn baby? He's three days old,
he's supposed to scream.

                              LUIS

Ay, does he do it all day, or just once I come home?

                              MARÍA

Yes, Luis, all day. I have to care for and hear him all day.

                              LUIS

(*Suddenly gets up*) Well, if it's going to keep me up I'd better
make the best out of this. (*Seductively closes in on **María***)

                              MARÍA

Luis, not now, I have to take care of the baby.

                              LUIS

You always say that, María. Dammit, when are you going to
take care of me? Huh? Huh!? (*Storms out.*)

                              MARÍA

Luis!

                        (*End scene.*)

*Scene IV - A Bar. **Luis** enters angrily and sees **Pablo** sitting there getting drunk.*

LUIS

Pablo! *¡Mi amigo!* Finally, someone I want to hear from! (***Pablo** says nothing*.) Pablo, snap out of it, you drunk bastard.

PABLO

(*Calm and coldly*) So. How's the newborn baby? What did you name it again? Oh, yes, Luis Jr. How cute. (*Suddenly explodes and stabs **Luis** in the stomach*) It should have been my son, you traitor! My son! Pablo Jr. Not Luis Jr.! Pablo! Pablo! You knew I loved her when you got here, you bastard! But I didn't say anything because you are my cousin. My own flesh and blood. (*He stares at his bloodied hands*). I didn't say anything. Hmph. My own damn fault then. (***Pablo** wipes blood on his shirt and walks out as **Luis** dies. End scene.*)

*Scene V - Sofía's House. **Sofía** is comforting **María**.*

SOFÍA

Mi'ja, everything will be fine.

MARÍA

Mamá, he hasn't been back in a week.

SOFÍA

You know how men can be. He'll probably turn up sometime.

MARÍA

Do you really think so?

SOFÍA

Yes, m'ija. Men are like cats. They leave for a while and then
they come back as if nothing had ever happened. Like they
never left.

MARÍA

I just...

SOFÍA

Mi'ja, I remember when your father got mad at me. This was
long before you were born. He got so mad because I didn't cook
his dinner on time. He got mad and left for four days. And I
cried and cried and then he came back like nothing ever happened. That's when I realized that he only did that to try and get
the upper hand on me.

MARÍA

So what did you do?

SOFÍA

Nothing. Oh, he tried leaving again, but I didn't cry. I just realized that men are like cats. Don't worry about them because
they can fend for themselves.

MARÍA

Ok...

SOFÍA

Why don't you go out and try not to think about it? Come, I
need to go get some peppers. We'll go together.

MARÍA

I can go. By myself.

SOFÍA

You sure?

MARÍA

Yes, I'm sure. Besides, you're the one that said I should get out and forget about things.

SOFÍA

Ok, María.

(***Sofia*** *hands her a basket as lights fade.*)

Scene VI - *The Street.* ***María*** *is walking across the stage and* ***Pablo's*** *voice is heard from afar.*

PABLO

María! María!

MARÍA

(*To herself*) Not now...

PABLO

María! Long time! Hey, why the long face?

MARÍA

It's nothing.

PABLO

Come come, you can tell Pablo!

MARÍA

Nothing. Nothing's wrong.

PABLO

I can tell you're lying. What's the matter, huh?

MARÍA

Leave me be.

PABLO

Time of the month?

MARÍA

Leave me alone, asshole!

PABLO

Ok, ok I'll leave you alone.

MARÍA

(*Sternly*) Thank you. (*She walks quickly away from him until he interjects*).

PABLO

I've seen Luis.

MARÍA

(*Freezes*) What?

PABLO

I've seen your husband.

MARIA

What? Where?

PABLO

But you told me to leave me alone, remember?

MARÍA

Dammit, Pablo, this is serious.

PABLO

I'll let you go--

MARÍA

Please!

PABLO

Ok. (*Suddenly changing his mood*) I don't want to tell you.

MARÍA

What?

PABLO

I don't want to tell you.

MARÍA

Why not? (*Silence*) Why not, Pablo?

PABLO

Because of where I saw him.

MARÍA

Where?

PABLO

María, this isn't going to be easy.

MARÍA

Where!?

PABLO

(*Long pause*) I saw him across the river--

MARÍA

And!?

PABLO

With...another woman.

MARÍA

(*Long pause*) W-what...?

PABLO

I didn't want to be the one to tell you.

(**María** *buries her face in her hands and runs out, dropping basket.* **Pablo** *picks up basket and walks the opposite direction, whistling.*)

Scene VII - *Night by the river and crickets are chirping.* **María** *enters with a wrapped blanket, she is still sobbing.*

MARÍA

Luis, if you don't want the baby, then I don't want the baby! If you don't want a life with me, then I don't want to live!

(*She very slowly carries the baby into the river with her and lights fade as she enters the water to drown herself.*)

Scene VIII - *Sophia's House. She is kneeling center stage, praying.*

SOPHIA

Lord, watch over her soul. Please, God, take care of her, she didn't know what she was doing, she didn't know what Pablo did. Lord, help me as well. I miss her. Sometimes, late at night, I think I can still hear her crying down by the river.

(*Lights fade.*)

[FIN]

MICHAEL VERDERBER

POETRY

SELECTIONS

THAT NIGHT

She danced
> Deceitfully beautiful and proud
> The vixen who broke men's hearts

He danced
> Diabolically handsome
> A fiend who waltzed supremely

All admired
> The best-looking couple in the dance hall
> Though his feet did not match

Twirling around
> He spun her in the air as if by magic
> But then he brought the darkness:

Billowing smoke
> A sulphurous smell
> The dance hall in ruins.

AMY CUMMINS

LYNX IN OCTOBER

Darkness
penumbra in autumn
chimeras of incense
October is a dragon.

We are the issue of a spell
the result of some potion
wax runs down an altar
magic
Palo
witchcraft
Catemaco.

In an egg I see your face
on the fire a buzzard stew
a river of tortured souls
that sing your name in unison.

Death caresses your face with his scythe
his yellowed hands of bone
run playfully along your lips
but you cannot feel it.

A cloud of grass
expands my soul
the penitent stare of the saints
a path upon reflected rays.

I am cold
afraid of the night
afraid of the conjuring
of the image of black wings.

of the knife of uncertainty
of the lynx that sleeps beneath the mescal
of the purging of my spine.

Leviathan, I am home at last.

ALEJANDRO CABADA FERNÁNDEZ
[TRANSLATED BY DAVID BOWLES]

LINCE EN OCTUBRE

Oscuridad
penumbra en otoño
quimeras de incienso
octubre es un dragón.

Somos el producto de un hechizo,
el resultado de una pócima
la cera se escurre por un altar
magia
Palo
brujería
Catemaco.

En un huevo veo tu rostro
en el fuego, un caldo de zopilote
hay un río de almas torturadas
al unísono cantan tu nombre.

La muerte acaricia tu rostro con su hoz
sus manos de hueso amarillo
juegan con la comisura de tus labios
pero no te das cuenta.

Una nube de mariguana
expande mi alma
la mirada penitente de los santos
un camino en tornasol.

Tengo frío
tengo miedo a la noche
tengo miedo a los conjuros
a las imágenes de alas negras

al flagelo de la incertidumbre
al lince que duerme bajo el mezcal
al extirpar mi espina dorsal.

Leviatán, ya estoy en casa.

ALEJANDRO CABADA FERNÁNDEZ

IN THE BEDROOM

The woman in black cries,
attempts to sleep,
but sleep never arrives:
it is a crucified steed.

A rotten stench fills the bedroom
her pores imbibe oblivion
sulfur evaporates between the sheets.

The woman in black trembles:
at the foot of her bed
two small men observe her.
one caresses her feet with his tongue,

the other whispers erotic verse
and slides his fingers
between her puzzled labia.

"We are wizards of the North:
we want your flesh
we want your womb
we want your skull
we want your blood."

The serpent of deceit
stands her hair on end:
inert, mute, terrified,
she knows her time has come.

A red tear
slips from her shattered cave
amidst silence and nausea:
the rancid breath of fear curls round,
welcoming her.

ALEJANDRO CABADA FERNÁNDEZ

[TRANSLATED BY DAVID BOWLES]

EN LA ALCOBA

La mujer de negro llora,
intenta dormir
pero el sueño no llega,
es un corcel crucificado

un olor a podrido invade la alcoba
sus poros beben el olvido
el azufre se evapora entre las sábanas.

La mujer de negro tiembla,
al pie de su cama
hay dos hombres pequeños que la observan
uno le acaricia los pies con su lengua

el otro susurra poesía erótica
y le desliza los dedos
entre sus labios confundidos.

"Somos los brujos del hemisferio norte
queremos tu cuerpo
queremos tu vientre
queremos tu cráneo
queremos tu sangre".

La serpiente del engaño
le eriza sus cabellos,
sabe que es el fin
inerte, muda, aterrada

una lágrima roja
escapa de su cueva agrietada
entre silencio y nauseas
el hálito del miedo la abraza,
le da la bienvenida.

ALEJANDRO CABADA FERNÁNDEZ

MELANCHOLIA

A light year away from you:

I cannot understand
the opaqueness of your eyes
the petrified stone of your hands
the acid that slips through your lips.

Let us speak—
mountains have no legs
there are no clouds of atomic crystal
or trees with eyes that spit pure fire.

I cannot understand
the honey that streams from your breasts
the perverse serpent of your hips
the inferno you coax out of me.

You are the bastard daughter of the night
the opium smoke that curls from my fist
an archangel's wings and Lucifer's smile.

Let us speak—
the planets were not born in a second
there are no birds with titanium wings
or flowers with the hands of a poet.

I cannot understand
the erotic venom of your flesh
the mortality born of your steps
the perennial climax that shakes my bloodless soul.

You are the most addictive darkness
the Tartarus of my nights
the three-dimensional abyss that defies time.

A million light years away:

holograms and flesh flow together
planets and stars perish
gods become men
men become comets.

Let us speak...let us whisper naked within the cosmic womb.

ALEJANDRO CABADA FERNÁNDEZ
[TRANSLATED BY DAVID BOWLES]

MELANCOLÍA

A un año luz de ti

no puedo entender
la opacidad de tus ojos
la piedra petrificada de tus manos
el ácido que escapa de tus labios.

Hablemos,
las montañas no tienen piernas
no existen las nubes de cristales atómicos
ni los árboles con ojos que arrojan fuego.

No puedo entender
las mieles que brotan de tu tetas
la serpiente perversa de tus caderas
el infierno que provocas en mí.

Eres la hija bastarda de la noche
el humo del opio que escapa de mis manos
las alas de un arcángel y la sonrisa de Lucifer.

Hablemos,
los planetas no nacieron en un segundo
no existen los pájaros con alas de titanio
ni las flores con manos de poeta.

No puedo entender
el veneno erótico de tu cuerpo
la mortalidad que produces al caminar
el orgasmo perenne que sacude mi alma desangrada.

Eres la oscuridad más adictiva
el tártaro de mis noches
el abismo tridimensional que desafía el tiempo.

A un millón de años luz

los hologramas y las pieles fluyen
los planetas y las estrellas mueren
los dioses se convierten en hombres
los hombres se convierten en cometas.

Hablemos... conversemos desnudos en el útero del universo.

ALEJANDRO CABADA FERNÁNDEZ

EXISTENTIAL THANATOS

What lies beyond the stars?
She asked herself from time to time.

Her scaly skin glittered like an iguana's in the moonlight
Though she had no notion of an iguana,
Her breath was dry and cold like the soul of a dog
That cannot grasp the passing of time
Though she had no notion of a dog.

Loneliness stabbed at her innards.

Her surroundings were sublime. Outlandish trees encircled her,
dropping rich oval fruit, crooning eldritch melodies.
The weather was fair. Peace and fronds enshrouded turquoise lakes.
Rows of multi-colored flowers dotted a dreamy landscape
that not even Monet could have imagined.

But such serenity did not suffice, for she was completely alone.

Sad, desolate, abandoned—weeping consumed her.
Life germinated beneath her feet, filling every nook,
but she saw no reason for her own existence.
A buzzing hive of questions caromed through her thoughts.
She had no joy, no hope, no dreams, no mirrors...She was dead.

She walked north and south, lost herself east and west,
Searching for anyone, on chaotic quests. She felt herself sinking
Into a horrifying, living swamp where she was consumed slowly
Through tunnels with twisted talons and venomous teeth.
The vision haunted her in the darkest of nightmares...
Perpetual digestion in an abyss of loneliness.

Her three-fingered hands slowly wrinkled like prunes
At the typhoon of tears that wracked her body for days.
Her sky-scape loomed: a black canvas studded with stars,
a huge orange planet that floated in the void
with two moons clinging to its right.

One day she awakened with no will to live,
Her existence an ache in every joint of her squalid form.
Nothing mattered, not her utopian paradise, not her miserable life.
Of a sudden a great roar splintered the heavens,
And she saw, descending slow, an enormous metal being,
Fire curling from its sides.

From high above, the crew caught sight of the fragile entity
And they exclaimed in awe, "It's true! We're not alone!"
At the same time, smiling with a sigh, she whispered.
"I knew I was not alone."

ALEJANDRO CABADA FERNÁNDEZ
[TRANSLATED BY DAVID BOWLES]

TÁNATOS EXISTENCIAL

¿Qué hay más allá de las estrellas?
A menudo se preguntaba.

Su piel escamosa brillaba como las iguanas bajo la luna,
    pero ella no sabía lo que era una iguana.
El aliento de su boca era seco y gélido como el alma de un perro
    que no entiende el transcurso del tiempo, pero ella no sabía
    lo que era un perro.

La soledad apuñalaba sus adentros.

Su entorno era sublime, vivía rodeada de árboles estrambóticos
que le obsequiaban frutas ovaladas y que cantaban extrañas melodías.
El clima era templado y había lagos de turquesa cubiertos
    de paz y vegetación.
Hileras de flores de de mil colores pintaban paisajes de ensueño
que ni el mismo Monet alguna vez imaginó.

Toda esta serenidad no le era suficiente pues al final estaba sola.

El llanto la consumía, triste, desolada, abandonada.
La vida germinaba bajo sus pies saturando su entorno,
    mas ella no entendía su razón de ser.
Como enjambre de abejas, miles de preguntas revoloteaban
    en su cabeza.
    No era feliz, no tenía esperanza, no tenía ilusiones, no tenia espe-
jos, estaba muerta.

Caminaba hacia el norte y el sur, se perdía en el este y el oeste
    en busca de alguien,
y la búsqueda era siempre un caos. Sentía hundirse en un pantano
    que la absorbía
a los adentros de un ser terrorífico en donde era consumida lentamente
    a través de túneles
con garras perversas y dientes venenosos. Al menos así lo había

visualizado
en la más oscura de sus pesadillas...una digestión perpetua
en el abismo de su soledad.

Sus manos tridáctilas parecían pasas por el tifón de lágrimas que por
días castigaba su cuerpo.
Su cielo era una alfombra tapizada por estrellas y un planeta inmenso
de tonos anaranjados que flotaba a la intemperie con dos lunas al
costado derecho y anillos ultravioleta eran su paisaje astral.

Un día despertó sin ganas de vivir, su existencia dolía en cada
coyuntura de su escuálido cuerpo.
Nada tenía sentido, ni su paraíso utópico, ni su existencia miserable.
De pronto un gran rugido emanó de los cielos, y vio descender
lentamente
un gigantesco aparato metálico que echaba fuego por los costados

Desde lo alto, la tripulación observó a la frágil entidad biológica
y exclamaron con asombro: "¡Efectivamente, no estamos solos!"
Al mismo tiempo, ella sonrió y suspirando, dijo en voz baja:
"Sabía que no estaba sola".

ALEJANDRO CABADA FERNÁNDEZ

THE INBETWEEN

The gravel is cool beneath me
I feel the dew on my bare feet
It isn't day
It isn't night
All I hear are infants' cries

Here I lie
Stranded
The trees sway
No creatures to be heard
I hope they don't feel the weakness inside me

I've been left hopeless, on the side of this road
Where my only mother is the cold

I'd run but trees surround me
The baby is crying without fail
At least twelve hours have passed
And the sun has yet to be seen

I feel them all around
But they are no where to be found
It drizzles endlessly
But the puddles don't gather rain

I can feel myself going mad

I run in all directions as fast as I can
With only dew drops to sustain me
I have to get out of here fast

The farther I run, the louder the cries
Alas, I come to a clearing
With a bright light at the end
There stands an angel
From neither Heaven nor Hell

"Please Sir, tell me how to leave. I'm tired and hungry,
I'm becoming too weak."

He rose slowly
And looked up at me sternly
Peering over me

"What have I done to deserve this?"
I plead

"It's not what you've done, but what you haven't."

Welcome to Purgatory
Private Hell

ALEXANDRA SEPÚLVEDA

WHAT GOES BUMP IN THE NIGHT

Fear the man who can see in the dark
Fear him for he sees the evil in your heart
He knows what goes bump in the night
He can see where you have no sight

Fear the man who can see in the dark
For your weakness is his strength
And the unholy are his closest friends
He sits at the foot of your bed
Or he'll peer through the closet instead

Fear the man in the dark
Because he does not need light to stalk

ALEXANDRA SEPÚLVEDA

CARRION FLOWER

When she opened her mouth to speak
Of rotten meat it would stink.
Everyone shielded their noses and eyes
And asked each other what had died.

"It must be poor hygiene!"
Cried one onlooker.
"It must be poor health!"
Shouted another.

After passing glares and lingering stares,
A child finally went to ask
"'Miss, why do you smell?"

"Young one, if you must know,
It's because I live in my own private hell—
I am dead inside.
Please don't tell."

ALEXANDRA SEPÚLVEDA

MY TENANTS .

I was asked today
If I wanted to pray;
I graciously denied
Because I harbor demons inside.
"But that is why!"
Cried the man gone blind.
Sir, I cannot pray.
I shall not pray
Because then my demons would leave.
And although it is on my soul that they feed
It's a small price to pay,
To never be alone again
Everything, no matter how ugly or evil,
Needs a place to call home—
Better my soul, than to roam.

ALEXANDRA SEPÚLVEDA

A RIVER'S TALE

I rage and whip
At the embankment
Within the confines of my retreat
Hushed whispers in fright
Tell about a lady
Who incessantly searches for her children
Along the edges of my stream

Low tide or high
She searches,
Gliding by and peering over the edge
With a tear-stained complexion
And a look of fear upon her face
She releases a moan of despair
While I continue at a gentle flowing pace
She releases guttural laments
When I move through with heavy pressure

I, too, face devastation
As I am not allowed rest due to her movements and cries
She is restless within hours of dawn to daylight
Unaware of her children's whereabouts, she searches on and on
Her punishment is a life spent by my side
Searching for her children
She calls their name and moves on and on

150 | ALONG *the* RIVER III

This lady lives a life of misery
Apparent by her relentless mission
It leads her nowhere
She fades away
Reappears
And lingers on and on

JOHANNA RIOS

SUPRISES FROM THE GRAVE

all dead bodies
were once like our own
with a wind in
their spirit, with
a fear for the unknown.

some say it is
unnatural to think
about death.
> but it comes most
> naturally when you
> feel most near it
> with thoughts
> and acknowledgments
> of what may come.

one never knows
exactly when their
time will come, unless,
if like la viejita
from la novela, you
can see- or know of
someone- who can
see into the future.

clairvoyance.
now wouldn't that
be nice?

there are so many
things to be done
with dead bodies,
that sometimes the
living find their dead
most dreadful.

not all things dead
have bodies to bury,
or spirits to lose,
or rotting to decay.

i tell you from
first hand experience
that a day (hopefully
you chance that day)
will come when you
realize the grave inside
your living insides
is the grave most
unnatural because
it can never die.

someday, taken for
granted, it will
descend upon you and
will come back to you.
it will harvest your
swollen spirits
and it will pull you aside.

this grave has filled
your silences with
moments most troublesome
and spontaneous, they
have made you
most miserable, and
have doubtlessly
changed your mind.

this grave is full
of weak voices
and even stronger
details, and surprises,
you once set aside.

and unlike most dead
bodies, this one lingers,
as it passes on.

PRISCILLA CELINA SUÁREZ

PEPE, WHO DIDN'T KNOW
DEATH WAS HIS TO TAKE

a dragon tattoo on his left arm
shifts into place
as Pepe relaxes his shoulders
      when he sees
      how I notice him.
in his eyes,
chismes strain to live
and with a fire, he speaks
      as he has never been heard before.
      Desire in me runs
      to smooth his greasy black hair down –
      tousled by thoughts of how, for sure,
      this visit would come.
I consider pulling at his chin
when he rubs his goatee
and his sunglasses fall out of place.
      but it is in the glaze
      of his eyes – white, all white...

he realizes we never met in life
when I startle
with his two step advance;
but despite my sudden shock
      and awareness, he asks me
      why I recognize him.

"The talk, the chismes, the people we share," I tell him,
"is how we meet in this moment's dream."
      I strain to hear his thoughts
      and wonder if Pepe
      is truly the angry cholo
      he was infamous to be.
his blackened lips speak words wiser...

why does the dead man
choose to take form
in my dreams?
      so vivid the memory.

PRISCILLA CELINA SUÁREZ

ECHOPLEX

Before they arrive they have already been out for sixty plus days
Days spent staying up late
Nights spend daydreaming about their social lives
Reading Facebook for updates about exes
Sneaking off and going on forbidden adolescent trysts
A youth misspent when I wished they would have
    read books instead
Some have kicked and screamed all their short lives
    at the system
I get it
At times I am still that awkward 7th grader among
    judgmental adults
Pimply and gangly...some are...
Unassuming girls dealing with embarrassing body issues...odors
Some strive to be noticed by their peers
But my only hope is they notice me
For now the halls are eerily quiet...empty of the very beings
    this echoplex was made for
My quiet steps lightly tap freshly waxed floors
The quiet before the storm.

ANNA L. SOLÍS

KEEPER OF FLIES

"En la boca cerrada no entran las moscas"
—Spanish Proverb

Strangest of the two
Walking down halls without floors
Stumbling quickly into unforgiveness
Forgiving the lowly
Women who smack their lips
Flies enter through bright, red doors...
Where modesty goes to die
Someone's reputation decays with their spewing lies
Secret glances foretell a drama...
Novellas played out as soon you turn your back
    to leave the room
Classless women oblivious to their own macabre witchcraft
Beauty is a child that plays fairly and loves thy neighbor;
    cursed for having a mother who is the keeper of flies
Good women locked up in closets, beaten by men,
    raped by cowards, found in basements
Good women, the beekeepers of life
They, the pinned butterflies in glass cases,
    unable to fly away from strife.

ANNA L. SOLÍS

THE DORIAN GRAY OF HER TIME

Poised there in all her naked glory to see
A muse shimmers for the artists
She is quite coy
Gently draping white linen
Like curtains that secure the privacy of a home
Intact, save for a fresh scar on her wrist
Shall she shine?
Project whimsical fantasies through her eyes?
Perhaps today she was in a mood and glared at the creepy visage
    of some of the artists
Artist who want to take her in and duplicate an image
The Dorian Gray of her time
Growing strangely younger
While projecting sins on the canvas
And soon her scar fades
She is immaculate

ANNA L. SOLÍS

THE RESURRECTION

A stretch of beach overlooking
the Laguna Madre she stands alone,
watching untamed waves. Her hair
glistens like black diamonds as the
wind swirls and sways the bright sun.

Off in the distance seagulls are flying.
They pass her by as they continue patrolling
the beach. The squawks and flapping of wings
fade and pass into nothing. With a grave look
she stands, searching the tides rolling in.

Gentle waves christen her feet
On the other side of the lagoon thrives
an eternal city. An endless city of revolts
of light and darkness, but neither wins
they only revolve and coexist.

A body is swept ashore. The water retreats.
The body is left behind. She runs to it, and lying
face down she turns it over. The face is hers,
the body is her own. She waits no more.
Her soul rejoins her body, searching no more.

WILLIAM MAINOUS II

DEMONS

Violent rains are falling. Lightning cracking
thunder rolling, thunder roaring over *el valle*.
Sky is trembling as dark darkness drowning!
Speeding, screeching as they plague the sky
howling madly, insanity, haunting! Though
on fire they are not consum'd. Wind is cold
coldness tearing! Will this wild brutal night
ever end? Hopelessly lost in our homes as
storms 'n' demons come charging cruelly, yet
  as night to day, all evil is passing, passing.

Warmth returns as silence comforts the air
calms. The fierce force is over. We are safe.
We tell 'n' retell stories of the ruinous night
build 'n' rebuild in any vacant places we find.
While far away dismal mixing taking place far
away dreary meetings of warlike preparations.
  Moving near, can't you hear them growling?!

Terror, terror, terror rages round my soul!
Panic, panic, panic as demons dart 'n' dash!
Race, race, race devils fleet 'n' flash furiously!
Swift, swift, swift 'n' speed the mad monsters
haste 'n' hurry, stop! Two grab my arms the
evil beasts so cruel 'n' vicious so cold 'n' vile
lift me up, a third claws 'n' slashes my chest in
half 'n' rips out my heart. We are let go I see its
  last beats. As we drop all drops to silence.

WILLIAM MAINOUS II

VIOLENT SPECTER

House plagued by a spectral burden,
Once flesh now a malevolent parasite
Rose out of a coffin after death of sanity.

No exorcism can appease the accursed presence
Nor can the rabid spirit be restrained
From slamming doors and breaking through walls.

Banshee cries and shattered glasses heard in halls
Countless nights without silence
No dreams for struggling sleepers.

Long since it lost all senses
No remorse, no sympathy, no humanity,
All gone from lethal consumption.

Born with high expectations, but never achieved.
Now dead and haunting a broken home.

DIANA ELIZONDO

VAMPIRE KINGDOM

They hold our existence in sickly pale hands
Never spare the weakest of society
Predators in suits and deceiving smiles.

Draining our essence 'til we cease to live
Stripping our rights; reduced to livestock
As they consume their bounty with bloody greed.

Spitting lies at their prey from both sides
No monster is exempted from centuries of affliction
Your dedication's worthless to infernal gluttons.

Dwelling in white palaces, staring down with hungry glares
Mindless, broken mortals prepared for endless feasting.
Lugosi's corpse rolling in shame.

The human herd, too deceived and dumb to revolt
Undead worshipped and guarded under the sign of freedom
A monument of a stake, such atrocious irony.

Ill-fated mortals produced, never born
In the cruel kingdom of vampires.

DIANA ELIZONDO

JACK O'LANTERNS

A bottle grenade flung inside
Glass eyes and wide mouth lighten by ember.
A quick procedure in making wooden faces shine.

Pumpkins aren't convenient enough these days
No damned spirit would fear a wee flicker.
Ridding ghosts demands greater craftsmanship.

There are other hollow canvases needing to be filled.
True beauty comes from orange and red blaze.
Such masterpieces created once a year.

Every sidewalk decorated with giant bright smiles.
Fiery chaos required for artful nights.

DIANA ELIZONDO

TO POE

Hope the abyss was kind to bring eternal rest
From vulgar sadness, unachieved hopes and maddening fears
Freed from the progress of physical and mental decease.

May Death reunite lost loves in permanent embrace
Know your dark muse had succeeded her purpose
Years of bleeding ink and spilling torment not in vain.

Happiness absent in tales of death and woe
Haunting minds with vengeful cats and hideous hearts.
Ominous ravens forever imprinted in history.

Dedications through black plums and blood petals.
Written hardships will never be forgotten.

DIANA ELIZONDO

THE GODS ARE FUNNY THAT WAY #6

for PL

I have made love to a woman
I loved in the Rio Grande
in deep South Texas, in a
lonely place, where we could
see no vast romantic vistas
but we weren't paying much
attention to romantic vistas

The water was not too cold
in August, the current up to our
shoulders not too strong that
our bare feet could not hold
to the bottom. There are certain
problems to making love in
a river flowing that I'll leave to

your discovery. They are too
private to go into here. Still, a man
might say that having made love
in the Rio Grande to the woman
he loves and loves him back might
be enough to carry him through
all the remains of his rough days—

even if she left him decades ago

CHUCK TAYLOR

BLUE 'N' BROWN IS BROWN

for Gil

ol' blue eyes
gave ol' one eye,
with pure mystical horse shoe luck,
to priestess
under rack of skulls
thinkin' he was helpin'
wipe out the pagans . . .

Now we raise our
Fists cryin'
"*viva la raza*"
smugglin' our herb
we take ol' blue eyes toys,
cans of raid for the roaches,
n' spray 'em down
with pride.

JUVENTINO MANZANO

AT THE PARK

Chicanos—
3 *chicanas* actually and 1 *chicano*
but the masculine in Spanish eliminates
those young high-school girls right on out of the picture
even though they were the ones in the frame
for their overheard comment—
one gestured to the east over my son and I scrunched
    in the dirt playing marbles
"There's a pisser—boys on the left, girls on the right"
as we sat under line of sight
and as they passed by
the *Virgen de Guadalupe*
on the back of black t-shirt
was a bleeding scar vagina__

JUVENTINO MANZANO

WHY I'M BECOMING CATHOLIC

I just realized that I do not have any friends, and it is because of this fact that I must become Catholic.

This morning, while in the shower, the urge to pee hit me. Standing there, I blinked and blinked again as I realized the stream from between my legs that splattered on my thighs and hit the tub, was not its usual light yellow color, but was in fact blood. I was peeing blood.

I splashed water on my thighs and moved the showerhead around to push the rest down the drain. I stuck my index finger inside thinking perhaps I had been mistaken and it was merely my period arriving early.

No.

Nothing.

Clean.

I had just peed blood.

What do I do?

I cannot tell my mother. No doubt she would call an ambulance. "It's cancer! It's a tumor!"

It's not a tumor, Mother!

I cannot call my girlfriends. Their interpretation of "please don't tell" is "as soon as we hang up, send out a massive text to everyone you know, making sure to give them every detail times two!"

No.

My friends won't do either.

I could tell my therapist.

No.

I can't tell him either.

He knows I've stopped eating. He knows I'm dizzy, tired, and my hair is falling out. When I first told him that I had stopped eating to lose weight he forced me to the doctors, like it was his personal mission to have me committed for an eating disorder. And then there was that time I slept with that seventeen-year-old boy and he threatened to call CPS on me.

No, I can't tell my therapist.

What can I do?

I have just peed blood. My only choice it to become Catholic. In that quiet booth behind closed doors, there is the only place where secrets are truly kept.

Yes.

I must become Catholic.

Forgive me father, for I have sinned. I'm dying to be thin.

NINA MEDRANO

CROW, BUZZARD, HUMMINGBIRDS

Crow was in trouble. Thoughtless and arrogant,
He had blundered into Buzzard's demesne,
The vast, bony desert where moribund mammals
Surrender themselves to heat, sand and beak.

Buzzard watched him from thorny green heights,
Jaundiced eyes glowering, two rotten suns,
And when Crow fluttered down upon a bloated corpse,
The scavenger spread its ragged wings to spiral close.

Startled into fluttering black by the feel of talons,
Crow couldn't twist the tarnished coil of his body:
His sable beak was pressed into dead flesh
As rapier pecking pierced his ancient hide.

Unaccountably, a charm of hummingbirds,
Blue-green blur of thrum and whistle,
Streamed by like filtered liquid sunlight,
Redolent of popcorn flowers and pulsing with joy.

Buzzard, startled, loosened its avid grip,
And Crow flipped onto his back, clawing
At the scavenger's belly, snapping at its wings,
Dismembering the fiend in a few fierce seconds.

Crow stood and watched the hummingbirds
As they swooped at blooming cactus arms.
"I want a tribe like that," he cried. "I want a flock
That will move as I move, think as I think!"

He looked about at the chunks of steaming flesh:
An idea wormed its way out of his nut-like brain.
Yanking plumes from his own black breast,
He planted each in a bloody bit of Buzzard.

Crow spat on the chunks, cawed himself hoarse,
Rolled them together and squatted down
Like a female warming her precious eggs
Until beneath him came a squirming chirp.

Soon six black fledglings were begging for food
And Crow slipped them slivers of bitter bird.
Laughing, he thought of the mischief they'd cause,
"A murder I'll call us, to mark our start."

DAVID BOWLES

CONTRIBUTOR
BIOGRAPHIES

Álvaro RODRÍGUEZ

has been writing since childhood and claims, in fact, to have done his best work when he was 11. With filmmaker Robert Rodriguez, he is the co-writer of the wishing-rock children's movie SHORTS (2009), and MACHETE (2010) starring Danny Trejo and Robert DeNiro, and is the screenwriter of the vampire western FROM DUSK TILL DAWN: THE HANGMAN'S DAUGHTER (2000). He is presently on the writing staff of the TV show FROM DUSK TILL DAWN. His short stories (including a Pushcart Prize nominee) have appeared in *The Mesquite Review, flashquake, BorderSenses, Popcorn Fiction* and other venues.

ALEJANDRO *Cabada* FERNÁNDEZ

is a Mexican poet and writer of short fiction. He is the author of the collections *Escarlata: Un libro de poemas* (2010) and *Días de púrpura* (2012), both published by Editorial Campamocha. His work has also been published in various anthologies and literary journals in Mexico and the United States. Proud of his Mexican roots, he promotes the Spanish language in the Rio Grande Valley of Texas through his writing and music. Recently, Alejandro wrapped up work on his Master's thesis in Spanish literature at the University of Texas Pan American.

Brianda SALINAS

It goes without saying, she goes without saying. Twenty-something, in love, an optimist, minimalist and when the mood strikes—a lady. Currently attending the University of Texas Pan-American to be a secondary English teacher. She has been Published in "Along the River II." She is a woman of many shades—always learning, always morphing.

MARIO *E.* MARTÍNEZ

Raised on unhealthy doses of samurai movies, horror flicks, spaghetti westerns, and Conan the Barbarian comic books, Mario E. Martinez began his storytelling career early in life. He currently teaches English at his hometown university in South Texas, where he lives. His short stories and poetry have been published in *Collective Exile: A Literary Magazine*, *Reflections*, *Turbulence*, *The Love of Writing*, and the *Laredo Morning Times*. His novel, *Twin Burials*, and short story collection, *San Casimiro, Texas*, were published by Authorhouse.

Angelo BOWLES

is the author of the locally popular children's series *Swift the Cat-Human*.

Evangelina AYON

was born in the Mexican state of Nayarit before relocating with her family to the Rio Grande Valley shortly thereafter. Growing up in a Spanish-speaking household, she learned to speak English from peers at school and quickly developed a love for reading and writing in both languages. That passion led her to persue a degree in English from the University of Texas Pan American. Today her main focus remains on sharing the unique cultural dynamics that exist on the Mexican-American border, with the rest of the world.

Tiffany CANO

Born and raised in Edinburg, Texas (loves her hometown), Tiffany is a senior at the University of Texas Pan American, pursuing a degree in English with an emphasis in Creative Writing. After graduation she would like to begin teaching or work in book publication. In her spare time she enjoys reading and writing mostly fiction.

ALYSSA *Aide* VELA

is currently in the MFA program with UTPA. She teaches Art Appreciation in La Joya, TX. She loves all things concerning stories and words and performance. Her work explores women, independence, judgments placed on women and the magic that is women.

PRISCILLA *Celina* SUÁREZ

Priscilla Celina Suárez, co-author of the 2012 Texas State Library's Bilingual Programs Chapter, is a native of the Rio Grande Valley. She has been published in the *Texas Teens Read!* Manual, the *Young Adult Library Services Journal*, and ALA's programming book *Cool Teen Programs under $100*. Her work can also be found in VAO Publishing's *Juventud! Growing up on the Border: Stories and Poems.*

ANNA *L.* SOLÍS

is a teacher and author from the Río Grande Valley.

Magaly GARCÍA

is a student at UTRGV with a major in English Creative Writing. Her hobbies include watching series, overanalyzing stories, and creating fictional works in order to expand ideas presented to her in her readings. When she isn't working or doing homework she spends her time daydreaming about all sorts of character and plot development for her next story.

Nina MEDRANO

Nina (Medrano) Bone is a student at the University of Texas-Pan American. She is working on her MA in English Literature and her Certificate in Mexican American Studies. After she graduates in December of 2014, she would like to continue her education and obtain an MFA in Creative Non-Fiction and Young Adult Anti-Bullying Literature.

Marianita ESCAMILLA

earned a BS in Biology, an MA in Literature at the University of Texas Pan American. She worked as a forensic scientist (DNA analyst) for the Texas Department of Public Safety for three years. Today, she is a Lecturer at the University of Texas Pan American, where she teaches Freshmen Composition and Sophomore Literature classes. Her research projects include ethnography studies. In keeping with her love of horror and forensic science, Ms. Escamilla presented the lecture "Staling the Silk: Serial Killer Fantasies and Realities" at South Texas Horror Con. She is the Editor-in Chief and founder of the creative writing online journal, *The Left Hand of the Father*.

Diana ELIZONDO

has spent most of her life in the Rio Grande Valley. An enthusiast for classic literature and the horror genre, Diana's works are influenced by Edgar Allen Poe, Emily Dickenson and Robert Browning as well as scary stories and folklore. Her poems are published in UTPA's *The Gallery 2012, Along the River II: More Voices from the Rio Grande* and the online literary journal *La Noria*. Diana received her Master's degree in English at May 2013 and is now working to get a M.F.A. in Creative Writing and become a well-known poet and a professor.

William MAINOUS II

holds a Bachelor's of English from University of Texas Pan American (2011) and is currently seeking a second degree. He is from and lives in Edinburg, Texas.

Susanna GROVES

A journalist and media associate with the Diocese of Brownsville, Groves is also president of the longstanding writers' group *Valley Byliners*.

Juventino MANZANO

grew up in the Rio Grande Valley. He has been writing for most of his life. His publications include the literary magazines of UT Pan American, the former Southwest Texas, and Illinois State University. At Illinois State he had the honor of studying creative writing under Ricardo Cortez Cruz and David Foster Wallace. He was nominated for the Push Cart award for poetry in 2008 and 2012. Other publishing credits include *Along the River 2, the Post Amerikan, Celebrate the Self, Armageddon Buffet, Poets wear Prada. Propergander, Le Petite Bourgeoisie, Last Stop at Union Station*, among others. He has self-published various works and is currently working on a novel of narco culture in the Rio Grande Valley and Northeastern Mexico as well as a collection of 25 years of poetry and a graphic novel adaptation of one his stories.

David BOWLES

credits his love of language, folklore and history both to his upbringing in a Mexican-American/Southern family and to the linguistic and storytelling gifts of his grandmother Marie Garza. In August of 2013 Lamar University Press published *Flower, Song, Dance: Aztec and Mayan Poetry*, a collection of Mesoamerican verse he has translated. He is the author of several other books, among them *Creature Feature: 13 Frightening Folktales of the Río Grande Valley* (2013), *Mexican Bestiary* (2012) and *The Seed* (2011). His editing credits include the magazine *Flashquake, La Noria Literary Journal*, the *Along the River* anthology series, and the reissuing of *Stories That Must Not Die. Top Shelf*, his book review column, is published each week in *The Monitor*, a regional newspaper.

Michael VERDERBER

is a lecturer of English at Texas A&M University - Kingsville and Artistic Director for the Kingsville, TX-based Zero Untitled Films / Productions. He has directed several theatrical productions with the company. A recent adaptation of Shakespeare's "The Rape of Lucrece" was performed in 2011 and an adaptation of the Bard's "The Phoenix and the Turtle" performed street theatre style in London, England.

Amy CUMMINS

lives in Edinburg, Texas, and teaches at the University of Texas Pan American.

Alexandra SEPÚLVEDA

is from the Rio Grande Valley with deep Mexican roots. She is a writer, musician, and aspiring journalist. She is greatly inspired by her interest in the both factual and fictional macabre.

Johanna RÍOS

is currently an instructor with degrees from South Texas College and the University of Texas Pan American. Her interests, when not grading lengthy essays, involve devoting time to her family, reading, writing, shopping, scrap booking, and traveling.

Chuck TAYLOR

hopes that his writings will help people individually and help societies as a whole. His most recent book is *Magical, Fantastical, Alphabetically Soup: Prose Poems, Mini Stories, and Rants* (Pinyon Press). He's been a college professor, balloon clown, and bookstore operator, not to mention editor-in-chief for *Slough Press*.